NATURE'S
SCHOOL

The Role of the Wabash River
in the Early History of Peru, Indiana,
1829–1913

Ron E. Withers

iUniverse, Inc.
Bloomington

Nature's School
The Role of the Wabash River in the Early History of Peru, Indiana, 1829-1913

Copyright © 2013 Ron E. Withers

iUniverse books may be ordered through booksellers or by contacting:

iUniverse
1663 Liberty Drive
Bloomington, IN 47403
www.iuniverse.com
1-800-Authors (1-800-288-4677)

ISBN: 978-1-4759-6786-9 (sc)
ISBN: 978-1-4759-6788-3 (hc)
ISBN: 978-1-4759-6787-6 (e)

Library of Congress Control Number: 2012923664

Printed in the United States of America

iUniverse rev. date: 2/7/2013

Contents

Illustrations vii

Acknowledgments ix

Introduction 1

Early Inhabitants of the Area and the
    Founding of Peru 9

How the Wabash & Erie Canal
    Reshaped the Landscape 39

Railroads, Floods, and Disaster 69

Consequences 113

Bibliography 117

Index 125

Illustrations

1. Jesse Williams, chief engineer for the Wabash & Erie Canal

2. Map of the feeder dam at the east edge of Peru

3. Train coming into Peru on the raised railbed east of town

4. Peru in the mid-nineteenth century

5. One of the earliest flood photos of Peru, believed to be of the 1875 flood

6. Map showing how the raised railroad beds leading into Peru funneled floodwater directly into the town

7. Broadway and Canal Street intersection in the early 1900's

8. Elbert W. Shirk

9. Indiana Manufacturing after the 1913 flood. Note the high-water marks on the building.

10. Ben Wallace

11. Looking north from the ridge in South Peru

12. Wreckage of homes in South Peru

13. South Peru after the flood

14. Pamphlet used to promote flood control efforts

15. The Wabash & Erie Canal at the east edge of Peru in 2012

Acknowledgments

No book is ever the work of just one person. I would like to thank all the people who have helped with this one. My gratitude goes out to Nancy Masten, Betty Wilson, and Mildred Kopis of the Miami County Museum in Peru. They helped me find information, loaned me research material, and provided insight into the history of the area. I also want to recognize the inspiration I received from Dr. Jon Kofas. He helped me understand that history often lies not on a distant horizon, but at one's feet. I also wish to thank Dr. Annie Gilbert Coleman for introducing me to the subject of environmental history. She has spent countless hours helping me view history in a new way, correcting me when I wandered, and pushing me to see the relationship between humans and nature in a different light. Without her help, this book would not be possible.

Lastly, I want to thank my grandfather, Grover Cleveland Good, for the inspiration his memory has given me. He was one of the heroes of the 1913 flood in Peru and an early environmentalist. Despite the fact that he held no degrees or titles, when it came to understanding the link between humans and the Wabash River, he was probably one of the smartest men to ever explore its banks. I think of him every time I put a paddle in the water.

Introduction

I felt an introduction to this book was in order
because of the unusual way in which I have approached the history
of my hometown, Peru, Indiana. Please bear with me as I explain the
methodology that led me to pursue an understanding of why Peru
evolved as it did. If you begin to nod off, just skip to chapter 1.

My first contact with the Wabash River came at the age of five
when Peru, Indiana, experienced a flood. The flood of 1959 was average
at best, but in the eyes of a five-year-old boy who lived only a block
away from the river, average was not a word that computed. I went to
bed the night before the water came, secure in the knowledge that my
world was safe. I awoke the next morning to an altered landscape that
included a new swimming pool where my backyard had been just a day
before. My initial excitement over the new addition to our yard was soon
tempered as my mother led me onto the stoop outside our kitchen door.
From there I could see the river. It bore no resemblance to the river I
knew. The lazy, chocolate-colored ribbon had changed into a raging,
debris-filled monster. The banks that normally contained the river had
disappeared. The railroad yards that defined Peru's economic heart ran
alongside the river, but they had also vanished. There were no switch
engines or boxcars, no men with oily rags, none of the everyday noises

that normally accompanied my bacon and eggs each morning. There was only the hiss of the water as it churned up my world. It was an entirely new concept for me; the river was out of control! I turned to my mother, who was still standing there holding my hand, and said, "This was a dumb place to put a house." It was a revelation that introduced me to the lessons taught on the banks of the Wabash River, where songwriter Paul Dresser said, "*Oftentimes my thoughts revert to scenes of childhood, where I first received my lessons, nature's school.*"[1]

What historical lesson does the Wabash River reveal in "nature's school?" The relationship between people and water is part of the larger question of how people and the natural landscape around them are connected as well as the historical consequences of that interaction. Historians such as Marc Reisner, Richard White, Mark Fiege, and Ari Kelman have addressed the tie between water and Americans, revealing a tempestuous historical connection. While there have been many volumes written about environmental history in the western United States, there are far fewer works on the landscape created by the interaction of humans and water on a smaller scale; yet important historical lessons are to be learned there also. The connection between Peru and the Wabash River is a prime example of how environmental connections influence history.

Smaller rivers like the Wabash have been overlooked in large part because they lack the "vastness" that many people still associate with the word nature. Environmental historian William Cronon argues that if we put wilderness on a pedestal, we may develop a mind-set that diminishes the historical value of places, people, and events that are "less natural."[2] Cronon's essay "The Trouble with Wilderness or, Getting Back to the Wrong Nature" makes the point that the accepted way of looking at

---

1   Paul Dresser, *On the Banks of the Wabash, Far Away* (New York: Howley, Haviland, 1897).
2   William Cronon, "The Trouble with Wilderness or, Getting Back to the Wrong Nature," *Environmental History* 1, no. 1, (1996): 20.

nature tends to give higher status to some places while diminishing the importance of others. Yet, for every Yosemite or Yellowstone, there are multiple upper Wabash Valleys and Mississinewa Rivers. Which of these is more important to a fundamental understanding of the link between people and nature? Is a mountain more important than a swamp, a forest more vital than a park? People tend to think that nature has to be big and separate from people. This is a faulty concept that denies much of what surrounds us as being natural and thus limits our vision as historians.

The notion that humanity and nature are separate prevents us from seeing a tree in the forest and a tree planted along a suburban street as being equal in the natural world. Historian Elliot West has said that a frontier never separates things, it brings them together.[3] Nature acts the same way. We sometimes can't see the forest for the trees or, for that matter, the river for the water. Historians have begun to write with the intention of showing how the relationship between rivers and people can expand our definition of what is "natural." The biggest lesson is that separating humans from nature is both difficult and inappropriate. Water and people are part of the same environment.

Author Ari Kelman, speaking of the link between New Orleans and the Mississippi River, made the point that the relationship between a river and a city is reciprocal; they act on each other.[4] Attempting to draw a line between man-made space and the natural environment may, at times, be an exercise in futility. Human desire to make water an orderly thing dispensed from a faucet denies the true relationship between nature and man because nature has a way of bypassing the faucet. Chapter 3 of Kelman's book *A River and Its City: The Nature of Landscape in New Orleans* describes the interaction between the

---

3   Elliot West, *The Contested Plains: Indians, Goldseekers, and the Rush to Colorado* (Lawrence: University Press of Kansas, 1998), 13.
4   Ari Kelman, *A River and Its City: The Nature of Landscape in New Orleans* (Berkeley: University of California Press, 2006), 8–9.

Mississippi River and the people of New Orleans and stresses the correlation between human and natural landscape. During the yellow fever epidemic of 1853, which devastated the city, local leaders realized that control of the waterfront did not translate into control of the Mississippi River ecosystem. No amount of political power could drain the swamp or create the cooler temperatures necessary to control the disease. The people of New Orleans thought they controlled nature, but the line between New Orleans and the environment was imaginary. Thousands of people died, and the epidemic did not subside until the frosts of autumn ended it.

Other environmental historians, such as Mark Fiege and Richard White, analyze the Snake and the Columbia Rivers to show how landscape consists of an inseparable mix of both people and nature. The use of water from these rivers for irrigation, drainage, and electrical power illustrates the intertwining of humans and nature into what Richard White calls an organic machine. He cites the damming of the Columbia as an example of human attempts to make the river do "work other than its own," thus giving human beings an opportunity to live and work differently.[5] Writing about people and the river separately would be like "writing a biography of a wife, placing it alongside the biography of a husband and calling it the history of a marriage."[6]

Mark Fiege's book *Irrigated Eden* argues that no matter what we do to nature, it always responds. There are often unexpected consequences when humans attempt to alter nature. *Irrigated Eden* uses the irrigation system of southern Idaho and the Snake River to show how man-made "improvements" to natural environments form landscapes that are a little bit of both. Fiege uses the example of Lateral L, a

---

5   Richard White, *The Organic Machine: The Remaking of the Columbia River* (New York: Hill and Wang, 1995), 59.

6   Ibid., x.

man-made irrigation ditch that ended up looking natural.[7] The line between man-made and natural was blurred to the point that it was no longer relevant. Fiege contends that no matter how hard people try to change the landscape, nature has a way of altering the new environment, often in ways that make it even stronger than before.[8] Moss infiltrated irrigation ditches, an abundance of new vegetation led to rabbit infestations, and water seepage poisoned the land with salt. For every move the hydraulic engineers made, nature answered, leading Fiege to say that "the boundary between what the irrigators considered artificial and natural, domesticated and wild, grew hazy, indistinct, and sometimes disappeared altogether."[9] This echoes Kelman's Mississippi and White's Columbia. There is much to learn about our place in nature from the historical relationship between rivers and people. No matter how preeminent human technology seems to be, nature always fights back, creating an unintended landscape and opening new avenues for historical research. As William Cronon said, "Landscape is more than just a physical set of things, because those things are always entangled in webs of meaning that, often as not, take the form of myth. A landscape, in sum, is not just a place, it is a story."[10]

The story I want to address is the one between the Wabash River and the city of Peru, Indiana. Ever since the day the river intruded into my world, I wondered why Peru was situated in such a vulnerable location. Not only was the town astride the Wabash, it was less than a mile downstream from the junction with the Mississinewa River. As I got older and learned more about the history of the area, I wondered why so much of the legacy of the river was ignored. The Wabash & Erie

---

7   Mark Fiege, *Irrigated Eden: The Making of an Agricultural Landscape in the American West* (Seattle: University of Washington Press, 1999), 5–6.
8   Ibid., 9.
9   Ibid., 78.
10   Cronon, "The Trouble With Wilderness," 9.

Canal played a large role in the history of the town, but the significance of water to local history had all but disappeared.

All we ever heard about as children was the circus history of the town. Locals also ignored the importance of the 1913 flood, probably the most significant historical event in the town's history. If not for a tiny plaque marking the high-water mark on a building at the corner of Sixth Street and Broadway, I would never have known the flood happened. Why was the town built where floods could destroy it? Where exactly was the line between the river and the town? How important was the 1913 flood? Why would the town ignore this aspect of its past?

I found no good answers to any of these questions until I learned about the field of environmental history. The history of Peru is intertwined with the Wabash River, but I never found a way to understand the relationship solely from the traditional perspectives of economic, political, and cultural history. Three previous volumes, written by Arthur Bodurtha, Charles Stephens, and Brant and Fuller, provide written histories of Peru that address the past from one or more of these traditional viewpoints, but none of them gave satisfactory answers to my questions. It was only after I read the works of Cronon, White, Fiege, and others that I began to see a way to understand some of the reasons why the history of Peru unfolded as it did.

Peru was established as a result of the construction of the Wabash and Erie Canal. The resulting landscape that evolved was not one where humans and nature were separated, but a complex one in which nature constantly reasserted itself in a man-made environment. The result of my research is this book, which attempts to show the different ways in which the people of Peru saw the Wabash River, how faulty interpretations of their relationship to it resulted in unintended changes to the landscape, and how the 1913 flood was the ultimate consequence of those changes. People living along the Wabash in the 1800s understood the river in different ways and altered it accordingly. Their efforts produced unintended consequences, leading ultimately to the economic disaster caused by the 1913 flood.

Chapter 1 addresses the interpretations of the landscape of the upper Wabash Valley of both Native Americans and white settlers. The original Native American societies that inhabited the region integrated their cultures with the ebb and flow of the environment, but the introduction of white immigrants driven by the economic potential of the Wabash River fueled dramatic changes in how the river and surrounding landscape were perceived as the immigrants sought to control the power of the river. That desire led to the building of Peru in a questionable location just below the confluence of the Wabash and Mississinewa Rivers.

Chapter 2 explains how perception and reality in the upper Wabash Valley were not always compatible. Human technology, represented by the Wabash and Erie Canal, seemed to separate what was natural from what was man-made, but the line between the two often blurred when nature interfered in the form of flood, drought, and the encroachment of animals and vegetation that caused major problems for the operators of the canal and the towns along its path. The canal also introduced thousands of immigrants to the area. They cleared trees, dug ditches, and introduced tiling systems that altered the landscape and caused the Wabash River to react in unintended ways.

Chapter 3 addresses the consequences of the changes introduced along the upper Wabash Valley and how the 1913 flood finally forced the people of Peru to address their misperception about the place of the town in the natural landscape.

Chapter 4 reinforces the conclusions of many other environmental writers. It's impossible to separate what is man-made from what is natural without consequences. The landscape created along the upper Wabash Valley when the first Americans arrived with their shovels and plows contained elements of both. Even as the human interpretation of who controlled the landscape evolved, the river responded to human changes in ways both unanticipated and uncontrollable by the people of Peru. They assumed that they were in control, which led them to take the river for granted. As a result, when the Wabash rose up, the town of Peru paid the price. The outcome is an explanation that sheds some new light on how, where, and why the city of Peru, Indiana, developed the way it did as well as explain why nature is not defined by a lack of human presence in the landscape but is a consequence of the marriage between the two. My house on Second Street was not a "dumb" place for a home; it was perfectly natural.

CHAPTER 1

Early Inhabitants of the Area and the Founding of Peru

T HE EARLY HISTORY OF THE UPPER WABASH VALLEY AND THE story of how the city of Peru was founded show how the conventional Native American understanding of the landscape along the Wabash River underwent dramatic change in the early 1800s as American settlers began to move into the area, bringing with them a new perception of the Wabash River. While the original inhabitants of the land saw the river as a source of life and the center of much of their culture, white immigrants saw the river as a source of energy capable of driving an economic engine that could harness the resources of the upper Wabash Valley. This change in perception is illustrated by the political and economic machinations that led to the founding of Peru, Indiana.

Three major groups have inhabited the area where Peru, the seat of Miami County, now stands. The prehistoric mound builders were the first inhabitants of the Miami County area and deserve a place in the narrative because what little evidence we have of them points to a close relationship to the river. The next people to arrive were Native Americans of the mid-seventeenth century, the Miami Nation in particular. It is important to understand their relationship with the Wabash River because it was so different from the view of the third group to settle in the area, the white settlers, who dramatically altered the perception of the river and how the local landscape was used. Each of these groups understood the river differently, illustrating the varying ways in which the landscape of the upper Wabash Valley was interpreted by the people who lived there.

The first inhabitants of the area where Peru now sits left no written record but relied heavily on the river to sustain their culture and almost certainly influenced the belief system of the Native Americans who followed them. We do not know much about them except that they were prolific mound builders, hence their name. Archeological evidence supports the argument that their culture depended on the Wabash River and that they populated the area around present-day Peru.[11] Experts do not consider them Native Americans but rather a prehistoric society that came and went long before the introduction of the known Indian tribes to the region. Prof. Frank M. Setzler, in his report "The Archaeology of the Whitewater Valley," says: "we gain the impression that a gap of more than a century must have existed between the time of the prehistoric tribes and the invading historic tribes. The connecting link between historic and prehistoric man—the builder of the mounds—in Indiana is missing."[12] An 1888 report by the Indiana state geologist stated that the first inhabitants of Miami County "left but few monuments to perpetuate their memory. Occasional mounds are about the only earthworks and ... the greater part of them are in the southern part of the county."[13]

---

11 Arthur L. Bodurtha, *History of Miami County: A Narrative Account of Its Historical Progress, Its People, and Its Principal Interests*, vol. 1 (Chicago: Lewis Publishing, 1914), 19.

12 Frank M. Setzler, *The Archaeology of the Whitewater Valley* (Indianapolis: Historical Bureau of the Indiana Library and Historical Department, 1930), 43.

13 Ibid.

Evidence of their existence around Peru also remains in the stone tools and weapons they left behind. A large proportion of these artifacts have been found along the Wabash and Mississinewa Rivers, lending credence to the idea that these prehistoric inhabitants relied heavily on those rivers to sustain their culture.[14] When the Miami Nation moved into the area, they reused arrowheads, spearheads, and other implements that they found. Although there is no ironclad evidence of a link between the two societies, it is probable that the later Native American societies inherited some of the Mound Builders' cultural focus on the Wabash River as well as their tools.

The first societies in the region for which a historical record exists are Native American. The most conspicuous tribe in the historical record of the Peru area is the Miami Nation, a people who moved into the vicinity of modern-day Peru in the late 1600s. They were an agricultural society. A French account from 1718 noted the industrious nature of the tribe and commented that they raised "a kind of Indian corn which is unlike that of our tribes at Detroit."[15] The demands of a primarily agrarian culture made the Indians dependent on water, and the Miami tended to settle near streams and rivers, where the rich soil promoted a wide variety of plant life, making it easier to grow the crops on which they depended and catch the fish and wildlife that supplemented their diet. They were experts at growing numerous varieties of corn, along with melons, squashes, pumpkins, and gourds.[16]

While hunting and fishing played a role in the everyday lives of the Miami, the predominantly agricultural nature of their culture led to the establishment of large, semipermanent villages within the territories they controlled. Invariably, these settlements were near rivers. Before the

---

14　Ibid.

15　Reuben Gold Thwaites, ed., *Early Western Travels, 1748–1846* (Cleveland: Arthur H. Clark, 1904–1907), 375.

16　Stewart Rafert, *The Miami Indians of Indiana: A Persistent People* (Indianapolis: Indiana Historical Society Press, 1996), 12.

mid-seventeenth century, the tribe (actually a loose association of six subtribes) was concentrated mostly across northern Indiana and Ohio. A war with the Iroquois pushed them into northern Illinois and Wisconsin during the 1650s, but by 1680, the Miami returned to Indiana, settling along the upper Wabash Valley, where they spent the better part of the next one hundred years.[17] They called the river the "Wah-Bah Shik-Ki," loosely interpreted as "pure white."[18] This was in reference to the way the sun gleamed off the pristine limestone bed of the river in the days before agricultural runoff turned it into the brown ribbon that cuts through Indiana today.[19] It was also a term of respect for the river.

Rivers were an important component in the creation beliefs of the tribe, symbolizing the bond the Miami had with their environment. According to their creation beliefs, the Miami came forth from a pool of water known as *Sakiwayungi*, or the "Coming Out Place." The tribal name for the St. Joseph River at South Bend was *Sakiwasipiwi*, or "Coming Out River." It was there that they believed the first Miami emerged and established the first village.[20] In other words, the Miami believed they were born from the waters they used each day. Not only did the river provide the rich bottomland needed for agriculture and a source for food and transportation, it was endowed with a spiritual and cultural significance which transcended day-to-day uses.

Daily use of the river was a fundamental part of the Miami belief system. Richard White argues in his book that "the energy of the Columbia River was felt in human bones and sinews; human beings knew the river through the work the river demanded of them."[21] It was

---

17   Ibid., 27.
18   Arthur C. Benke, Colbert E. Cushing, *Rivers of North America: The Natural History* (Burlington, MA: Academic Press, 2005), 396.
19   French explorers to the area later corrupted the word to "Ouabache" and eventually the word became "Wabash."
20   Ibid., 15.
21   Richard White, *The Organic Machine: The Remaking of the Columbia River* (New York: Hill and Wang, 1995), 4.

the same for the Miami. The river was integral to their daily lives. One story in particular illustrates this relationship. There used to be a large rock in the middle of the Wabash River a few miles east of Peru near a spot known as Boyd's Park. The rock had a dished-in spot on the top of it that held about three gallons of water. According to Chief Clarence Godfroy of the Miami, a large Indian village was once there, and the Indians used the rock as a gristmill. "Indian corn was put into the hollowed out space … It was pounded into corn meal. Many meals were prepared for the Indians from the corn meal pounded on this rock."[22]

The tribe used this rock on a regular basis, literally standing in the water to pound the corn. The river and its landscape were part of their daily routine. They knew the river by their work and depended on it for both spiritual and temporal needs. The Miami Indians looked at the Wabash as a source of life. They fished and hunted along its banks and grew crops in the rich soil it provided. Because of their seminomadic existence, they were able to pick up and move when the river flooded. They literally tried to "go with the flow." Thus, the Miami culture found a balance with the moods of the Wabash.

The tribal view of the river was in direct contrast to that of the Americans when they came to the area. The Miami were intertwined with the landscape. White settlers in the area saw the river in a more detached manner. To them, the river was a power source for technology, not a source of cultural strength. One needs look no further than the name of the rock used by the Miami. To the Indians it was "gristmill rock," a place in the river from which they provided nourishment by working with what nature provided. Whites in the area knew it simply as "dishpan rock," for they could see no other use for a rock in the middle of the river. If a white man wanted a gristmill, he took the water from the river to power a machine that would make corn meal. The water was his to use because he could change the river and control it.

---

22   Chief Clarence Godfroy, *Miami Indian Stories* (Winona Lake, IN: Light and Life Press, 1961), 4–5.

The Indians felt the power of the river in the daily work they did and respected their closeness to it.

The settlers relied on technology to manipulate that same power, which distanced them from the river. They saw the river as a source of wealth. There was both economic and political power in abundance to be extracted from the flowing water. Instead of a force of nature, the Wabash was merely another tool they could bend to the will of industrial progress. Richard White's book points out that while through much of history work and energy have linked humans and water, there is little in modern life to maintain that connection because machines have taken over much of our physical labor, separating us from nature and giving us the false perception that we can control it. The only time we notice the power of nature is when it bites us.[23] In other words, ignorance and complacence about the relationship between people and nature often leads to disaster. This theory is significant in the development of the Wabash River in general and the political and economic history of Peru, Indiana, in particular.

Native Americans did not understand the white American's view of the landscape. They shared the same philosophy with the Sac chief Black Hawk who, in 1832, mocked a treaty with the Americans by enunciating his belief that land could never be sold by the Indians because "their lives and the land's were one."[24] He derided the American tendency to divide and order land into neat parcels to be bought and sold by stating, "Nothing can be sold but such things as can be carried away."[25] Unfortunately, for both Black Hawk and the Miami Nation, the Americans did not share the same viewpoint. By the 1820s, American desire for economic growth altered the river's place in the landscape as

---

23   White, *Organic Machine*, 4.
24   William Cronon, *Nature's Metropolis: Chicago and the Great West* (New York: W.W. Norton, 1991), 27.
25   Ibid.

well as the position of Native American peoples along the upper Wabash Valley.

The topography of the upper Wabash Valley made the territory along the Wabash River irresistible to pioneers looking to expand the economic base of the new country. By the early 1800s, white settlers had moved across the Appalachian Mountains and into what are now Tennessee, Kentucky, Ohio, and southern Indiana. The lack of roads made rivers such as the Wabash an integral part of westward expansion: "Rivers offered cheaper and more dependable transportation. The geology of the area reinforced the American proclivity to gobble up land. The best farmland bordered streams and many rivers produced a relatively flat alluvial plain that ... lent itself to the construction of towns."[26] Contact between humans and the river became more complicated with the arrival of farmers, merchants, and engineers, who saw the Wabash as a God-given hydrological highway, flowing for their economic use. The indigenous spiritual perception of the landscape was replaced by a new one based on the American spiritual belief that westward expansion was ordained by God, who provided natural resources as a means to that end. It made more sense to think of the United States at the dawn of the nineteenth century as "a series of rivers separated by land, than as a huge land mass punctuated by rivers."[27]

Early US leaders such as George Washington viewed rivers as economic landscapes and saw canals as an answer to the transportation woes of a fledgling United States. In particular, Washington saw the Wabash River as a way to connect the Great Lakes to the Mississippi River, opening vast tracts of land in the Northwest Territories to settlement and trade. Washington broached this idea in 1784 when he asked Congress to pursue the exploration of rivers "as far west as the

---

26   Donald J. Pisani, "Beyond the Hundredth Meridian: Nationalizing the History of Water in the United States," *Environmental History* 5, no. 4 (2000): 468.

27   Ibid.

Miamies, running into the Ohio and Lake Erie ... to see how the waters of these communicate with the River St. Joseph ... and the Wabash."[28] Indiana became a state in 1816, and by 1824 the Indiana legislature had funded the first surveys of a proposed canal along the Wabash River. The federal government pushed the plan forward in 1827 by granting 527,271 acres of land stretched over 160 miles of river to Indiana. The sale of that land would finance the building of the canal and provide the stimulus for economic expansion along the river corridor.[29]

The federal government was able to offer the land to Indiana because of a series of treaties made with the Miami, Potawatomi, and other tribes who lived along the Wabash River corridor. The road to those treaties had not been an easy one. The Indians had maintained parity in power with the French and British who first came to the western frontier. When warfare erupted, as often as not it was Native Americans who were victorious. It was not until the Indian defeat at the Battle of Fallen Timbers in 1794 that the negotiations began which resulted in the loss of most of the Indian land along the Wabash River by the end of 1826.

Those negotiations quickly eroded the Miami culture. After the Treaty of Greenville in 1795 evicted them from their villages in northeast Indiana, many of the Miami Indians relocated to small villages along the Wabash, Mississinewa, and Eel Rivers in or near what is now known as Miami County. They believed that they could live along the Wabash as long as they desired, but the move dispersed most of the tribe into smaller villages, which isolated them from the trade center of Fort Wayne where they could easily trade for the goods they needed.[30] Article V of the Greenville treaty also stipulated that if the tribe was "disposed

---

28 Paul Fatout, *Indiana Canals* (West Lafayette, IN: Purdue University Press, 1972), 23.
29 Thomas E. Castaldi, *Wabash & Erie Canal Notebook I: Allen and Huntington Counties*, 2nd ed. (Fort Wayne, IN: Parrot Printing, 2002), 2.
30 Rafert, *The Miami Indians*, 63.

to sell their lands, or any part of them, they were to be sold only to the United States."[31] While seemingly innocuous, this part of the treaty guaranteed that when pressure to sell the land became strong enough, the US government had the power to take it from the Indians.

By 1800, American pressure in the newly created Indiana Territory began to erode the traditional Miami perception and use of the landscape. A further series of treaties interspersed with military defeats along the Wabash and Mississinewa Rivers in 1811 and 1812 left the Miami Nation weakened and isolated both physically and culturally. By the time Indiana became a state, the other tribes in the region, with the exception of the Potawatomi, had already sold or abandoned their land. This left the Miami Indian land along the Wabash encircled by Americans and well behind the new western border of the frontier.

It also made their land a target for acquisition by whites as the burgeoning American economic system began to transform the landscape with new methods of transportation inspired by the internal improvements boom. "The Miami tribe occupied some of the most valuable potential commercial sites in the state, astride proposed canal and highway routes and at the location of future towns and cities."[32] The National Road, the Erie Canal, and other projects aided westward expansion and made the eastward movement of agricultural and manufactured goods from the western frontier easier. It was only a matter of time before the economic development of northern Indiana began.

Erosion of tribal life continued during the early 1800s as the Miami were maneuvered into a subsistence lifestyle on steadily diminishing land holdings. New American residents flooded Indiana, sweeping up land and redefining the landscape along the Wabash through treaties with the Native American inhabitants. Between the years 1800 and

31   Samuel Flagg Bemis, *Jay's Treaty: A Study in Commerce and Diplomacy* (New Haven, CT: Yale University Press, 1962), 42.
32   Rafert, *Miami Indians*, 88.

1816, the white population of the territory grew from about twenty-five hundred to almost seventy thousand.[33] By 1820, the number more than doubled to 147,178.[34] The rapid influx of settlers put massive pressure on the Miami way of life. While the tribe had spent the better part of the previous two hundred years immersed in a patchwork society that involved trade with French, British, and Americans, they had achieved a cultural equilibrium with Western Europeans that enabled them to survive in the natural landscape. They hunted, fished, and grew crops up and down the upper Wabash Valley while maintaining a belief system that had changed little over the years.

As Americans poured into Indiana, they decimated game populations, seduced the Indians with alcohol, and promoted new treaties that destroyed the longstanding cultural equilibrium. A series of treaties, culminating in the Treaty of St. Mary's, Ohio, in October 1818, chipped away at the traditional Miami society. Substantial annuities were offered by the federal government in return for Miami land, creating a new Native American economy that was dependent on the US government as well as fracturing what remained of Miami landholdings into six small village reserves and twenty-four individual reserves.[35] By 1820, traditional Miami society was substantially weakened.

The loss of most of their land, coupled with the introduction of a new economy, severely disrupted the Miami culture, altering their perception of the landscape. Instead of a trading system based on the furs and hides taken from the river valley, the Miami developed a dependence on the goods and services offered by the American traders. These businessmen poured into the area around Fort Wayne with the intention of obtaining annuity money given to the Indians by the

---

33   William Wesley Woollen, Daniel Wait Howe, Jacob Piatt Dunn, "Executive Journal of Indiana Territory 1800–1816," *Indiana Historical Society Publications* III, no. III (1900): 82.

34   John Brown Dillon, *A History of Indiana from Its Earliest Exploration by Europeans* (Indianapolis: Bingham and Doughty, 1859), 563.

35   Rafert, *Miami Indians*, 80.

federal government as part of various treaty negotiations.[36] The loss of so much of their land "separated the Miami from their hunting territories, fishing weirs …, and made other subsistence activities more difficult."[37] Government officials, white traders, and land speculators intent on reordering the river to fit a new purpose put great pressure on the Miami, causing the tribe to rethink their place in the landscape of the upper Wabash Valley. By 1826, it was apparent that Chief Blackhawk was wrong. Indians could sell their land.

The fact that the leader of the Miami at this critical juncture in their history was half white reflects the evolution of Miami culture and their changing position within the landscape. Their principal chief was Jean Baptiste Richardville, successor to Chief Little Turtle in 1815.[38] Richardville's father was a French trader, and his mother was the daughter of Little Turtle. He was raised as a Miami and knew their culture intimately but had one foot in the white world also. He developed a keen business sense from the American traders around him and "grew into an intelligent, shrewd man, wise in the ways of the white man's politics."[39]

Richardville was a savvy businessman and ran one of the largest trading posts at Fort Wayne in 1790. It was a place where Miami and American culture and landscape overlapped. Settlers built the original fort there because it was the location of Kekionga, the largest of the Miami villages. It was also the place where the St. Mary's River converged with the St. Joseph River to form the Maumee. The fledgling commerce center was both a transportation and financial hub for the area because the US government disbursed annuity payments there.

Richardville had stiff business competition in the form of white traders who were intent on bilking the Indians of their money and land.

36   Ibid.
37   Ibid., 85.
38   *The Indiana Historian* (November, 1993): 4.
39   Ibid.

Henry Hay visited Fort Wayne that year, and he observed: "Everyone tries to get what he can by fowle [sic] play or otherwise ... in short I cannot term it in a better manner than calling it a Rascally Scrambling Trade."[40] Richardville managed to survive and prosper there.

He also understood the value of money and land ownership in a way most members of his tribe could not. Arthur Bodurtha, one of the original historians in Miami County, had this to say of Richardville: "His Indian name was Pe-she-wa (the Lynx), a name indicative of his character—always alert and watchful for his own interests and the welfare of his tribe."[41] The 875,000 acres the tribe owned in 1820 spread across some of the most valuable land in the state. Richardville's knowledge of the American real estate system plus his trading expertise helped to make him an effective diplomat in treaty talks with the US government. General John Tipton, who was one of the federal negotiators for the Paradise Spring Treaty and a well known trader and land speculator in his own right, called Richardville "the ablest diplomat of whom I have any knowledge."[42]

By 1815, when Richardville became chief, he had already been a witness to the removal of other tribes from their lands, whether by treaty or force.[43] He knew the value of the land and realized that, one way or another, the tribe was going to lose it. Consequently, he used his skills as a negotiator to sell the Miami lands that remained along the upper Wabash Valley to the Americans in exchange for large monetary concessions.[44] Much of the money went to the tribe, but a large portion of it was awarded to Richardville and his family as an incentive to convince the Miami to vacate the land. He also received guarantees

---

40   Bert Joseph Griswold, Samuel R. Taylor, *The Pictorial History of Fort Wayne, Indiana: A Review of Two Centuries of Occupation of the Region About the Head of the Maumee River* (Chicago: Robert O. Law, 1917), 89.

41   Bodurtha, *History of Miami County*, 29.

42   Ibid., 233.

43   *The Indiana Historian* (November 1993): 4.

44   Ibid.

from the federal government that he would never have to leave his landholdings in Indiana. When Richardville died in 1841, his personal wealth was over $1,000,000, making him the richest Native American in the United States at the time. He owned vast tracts of land, numerous houses, and was rumored to have buried over $200,000 in coin on his various properties.[45]

Richardville inherited a very difficult position as leader of the Miami Nation, and his consequent actions reflect the changing perspective of the landscape the members of the tribe were experiencing. He oversaw the treaty negotiations and land sales that marked the time when the Miami came to relate to the river and its landscape in the same way as the whites, as property to be bought and sold. It's hard not to be critical of Richardville for selling Indian land at personal gain, but it's equally difficult to assign only one motive to his actions. He is sometimes called the "Man in the Middle."[46] Was he simply a greedy man who took advantage of his position to get rich, or was he a man who saw his native way of life dying and tried to help his people to the best of his ability?[47] It's a question difficult to answer, but there is no doubt that he presided over a time of great change within the Native American community along the upper Wabash Valley. While the mind-set of previous Miami leaders would have made them balk at selling the gristmill rock, Richardville knew enough of Americans to realize that the world of the Miami was changing with or without their consent. He sold the rock for as much money as possible and hoped his people could adapt and buy their corn meal like the Americans did. As historian Elliot West said: "Environmental history is, among other things, a lengthy account of human beings over and over imagining

45   John H. Stephens, *History of Miami County: Illustrated* (Peru, IN: John H. Stephens Publishing, 1896), 28.

46   *The Indiana Historian* (November, 1993):1.

47   Ibid., 4.

themselves into a serious pickle."[48] A pickle is exactly where the Miami Nation found themselves.

When the Miami signed the Treaty of Paradise Springs with the US government on October 23, 1826, the Wabash River Valley changed from the focal point of their culture into a commodity within the economic landscape being created by the new owners of the land. The Treaty of Paradise Springs removed the last roadblock to the economic exploitation of the Wabash River Valley. It called for the Miami Indians to give up most of their remaining land along the Wabash River and provided a right of way for the building of a canal across the few parcels that were left. In return, the tribe received over $31,000 in money and trade items (almost $750,000 in today's dollars) as well as a future payment of $41,259 in goods. The federal government also increased their yearly annuity to $25,000 and gave various chiefs money, cattle, homes, and sections of land.[49] Miami historian Stewart Rafert explains: "In the face of mounds of finery, offers of houses and private lands for the chiefs, and the flow of mind-dissolving hard liquor, the Miami relented and signed the treaty."[50] Richardville was the prime beneficiary of this largesse, receiving a home, trading concessions, and several sections of land (including the present site of Peru). Another Miami chief, Francis Godfroy, also received a section of ground directly east of Richardville's.

When the articles of this treaty went into effect, the Miami Nation's role within the Wabash Valley changed. The Americans had successfully redefined the purpose of the river and its surrounding landscape by turning it into an economic engine for the region. Gristmill rock was now dishpan rock. The traditional Native American interaction with

---

48   Elliot West. *The Contested Plains: Indians, Goldseekers, and the Rush to Colorado.* (Lawrence: University Press of Kansas, 1998), xxii.

49   Charles J. Kappler, ed., *Indian Affairs: Laws and Treaties,* vol. II (Washington DC: Government Printing Office, 1904), 278–81.

50   Rafert, *Miami Indians,* 93.

the river slowly disappeared. The Miami remained in isolated pockets, but their main role in the new economic landscape was as a magnet for white traders attracted by Indian annuity money.

The Paradise Springs Treaty marked a changing of the guard as far as the river was concerned. The Americans were now free to begin economic expansion all along the new corridor. The treaty opened a figurative floodgate as land speculators, traders, and businessmen moved into the newly acquired territory. The river was no longer seen by recently arrived inhabitants as a part of the natural landscape. It was a new source of wealth, there to provide transportation and power that would fuel a new economy and bring major fortunes to businessmen who were lucky enough or farsighted enough to take advantage of it.

By the early 1820s, the main congregating point for business entrepreneurs was the trading center for the upper Wabash Valley, Fort Wayne. The dispensing of federal annuity money there drew these men to Fort Wayne like flies to honey. There were no other towns at all along the upper Wabash River at this time, just a few Indian villages. One of the first Protestant missionaries to the area described Fort Wayne in 1820 as "a little village of traders and persons employed by the government as interpreters, smiths, etc. ... the nearest settlement of white people was ... nearly one hundred miles distant."[51] Captain James Riley, an engineer evaluating the feasibility of a canal from the Maumee to the Wabash, provided a more colorful description of annuity payment time at Fort Wayne in 1820. His description illustrates the collision of Native American and white culture:

> There were at least one thousand whites here from Ohio, Michigan, New York, and Indiana, trading with the Indians. They brought a great abundance of whiskey with them, which they dealt out to the Indians freely, in order to keep them continually drunk and unfit for business; their purpose being to get the best of them in trade." Horse-racing, gambling,

---

51   Griswold, *Pictorial History of Fort Wayne*, 244.

drinking, and debauchery, extravagance, and waste were the order of the day and night.[52]

The furious activity by traders and land speculators alike to relieve the Indians of their wealth and extend them enough credit to be able to confiscate their land when payments were due created a new economic landscape along the Wabash River. The year 1820 was pivotal for the young settlement. The federal government recognized the growing importance of the town that year when it established mail service there. By 1823, the first land office was opened for the purpose of selling the Miami holdings that were being accumulated by the series of treaties with the US government. Fort Wayne was a place where land and money seemed to be available in copious supplies.

Among the people flocking to Fort Wayne to make their fortunes were Joseph Holman and William Hood, the two men who would soon found Peru. The Hood family arrived from Dayton, Ohio, in 1822, and in early 1823 Joseph Holman was sent by President Monroe to be the first receiver at the Federal Land Office in Fort Wayne.[53] Both men were experienced in business and politics. With the sale of Indian land and the possibility of a new canal along the Wabash River as incentives, they moved to Fort Wayne to take advantage of economic and political conditions that converged there. They brought with them American ideas about the place of rivers within the new landscape. Before 1824, most whites recognized that most of the wealth gleaned from the region was in the form of pelts and furs brought in for trade there, making the economic system dependent on the traditional environment along the rivers in the area. By 1824, traders found it far more profitable to trade for the annuity money the Indians received than to depend on the supply of furs. Land itself became the most valuable commodity as speculators moved in, and the time was right to transform the upper

---

52   Ibid., 248.
53   Ibid., 261.

Wabash Valley from "part of the frontier into a product of it."[54] It was time for settlers to tame this newly acquired wilderness, and men such as Hood and Holman wanted to be the ones to sell them the land and the tools to make the change. Aided by wealthy speculators like the Ewing family, they would soon have their chance.

The Ewings personified the new breed of speculators, who used trading experience and political connections to create opportunity and wealth along the upper Wabash Valley. Colonel Alexander Ewing, his wife, four sons, and three daughters came to Fort Wayne in 1822. They quickly became an integral part of the political and economic fabric of the town. Ewing achieved his rank serving with General Harrison during the War of 1812. He was an Indian trader from at least 1787 and established a tavern, hotel, and trading post in Fort Wayne. According to Fort Wayne historian Bert Griswold, he acquired "real estate which is today of incalculable value."[55] Two of his sons, George W. and William G., were also well-established traders.

Historian Stewart Rafert documented their relationship with the Miami Indians. He stressed their importance to the history of the area because of the influence they had with General John Tipton, the man who became the Indian agent in Fort Wayne in 1823. Tipton was a good man to be close to because he controlled trading licenses and treaty negotiations.[56] The Ewings fostered the relationship with Tipton because it allowed them to use federal Indian policy for their own gain. Rafert points out that by the time the Ewings arrived in Fort Wayne, "they had thirty-five years experience in the Indian trade, which meant intimate knowledge of, but not necessarily respect for, the ways of the Indians."[57]

---

54 Harvey L. Carter, "Rural Indiana in Transition, 1850–1860," *Agricultural History* 20, no. 2 (1946): 107.
55 Griswold, *Pictorial History of Fort Wayne*, 255.
56 Rafert, *Miami Indians*, 90.
57 Ibid.

When Allen County was established in 1824, the first commissioners' meetings were held at Ewing's tavern; the Ewing home was the first meeting place for the circuit court, and Alexander was elected as one of three justices of the peace.[58] Charles W. became the first county prosecuting attorney, and his brother William became a lawyer. Alexander Ewing also purchased an additional eighty acres of prime real estate from the government in what would become downtown Fort Wayne for the sum of $100.[59] When Tipton resigned as Indian agent in September, Charles W. Ewing was named by Congress as his replacement. The Ewings were involved in virtually every aspect of the political and economic system on the Upper Wabash and provided a business model for other entrepreneurs coming to Fort Wayne. They were influential in local and state politics for years to come. Men looking to advance their fortunes were anxious to foster relationships with the Ewings.

One of the entrepreneurs who found his way to Fort Wayne was William Nesbitt Hood, a thirty-two-year-old merchant and trader from Dayton, Ohio. Information about his early life is rather scarce, but the rapidity with which he rose in Fort Wayne social and political circles implies that he came to the city as an established businessman with an aptitude for frontier society. An early history of Peru states that after his arrival in Indiana "he carried on a successful mercantile business, dealing extensively with the Indians during the time of his residence there [Fort Wayne]." [60] A Miami County history contends that Hood amassed a sizable fortune during his stay at Fort Wayne, which lends credence to the notion that he was an astute Indian trader.[61]

Hood quickly became involved in Fort Wayne politics and the

58   Griswold, *Pictorial History of Fort Wayne*, 265, 267.
59   Ibid., 263.
60   Brant and Fuller, eds., *History of Miami County Indiana* (Chicago: Brant and Fuller, 1887), 437.
61   Bodurtha, *History of Miami County*, 156.

purchase of land. In the first Board of Commissioners meeting held at Alexander Ewing's house in May 1824, Hood was appointed by the same body as inspector of flour, beef, and pork for Wayne Township. He also served with Alexander Ewing on the first grand jury called in August 1824 and became a justice of the peace alongside Ewing.[62] In September, Hood also bought a prime lot in Fort Wayne for a little over twenty dollars.[63] By 1827, he was designated a judge of the circuit court of Allen County by the governor of Indiana. Hood also married Charlotte Ewing, the daughter of Alexander Ewing, in 1827. Whether by accident or intention, William Hood developed the connections and the wealth needed to take advantage of the events taking place along the Wabash in the mid-1820s.

Another businessman who moved to Fort Wayne was Joseph Holman, who was born in Woodford County, Kentucky, on October 1, 1788. His family moved to what is now Wayne County, Indiana, in 1805, and he married there in 1810. He also served under General Harrison during the War of 1812 and built a blockhouse on his farm at that time for the protection of the local citizenry.[64] Joseph also made his living as a trader. His father had been a captive among the Indians for many years and was both familiar and friendly with many of the regional tribes. It wouldn't be much of a stretch to think that the father passed on some of his knowledge of Indian language and customs to his son. Whatever trading skills Joseph possessed, he was soon wealthy and became heavily involved in politics. He was a candidate for the territorial legislature in 1814 but lost the election by one vote when he neglected to vote for himself. His opponent passed away before the session started in 1815, and Holman was picked to fill the seat. He

62 Griswold, *Pictorial History of Fort Wayne*, 266–67.
63 Glen A. Blackford, ed., *The John Tipton Papers*, 3 vols. (Indianapolis: Indiana Historical Bureau, 1942), I, 405.
64 Griswold, *Pictorial History of Fort Wayne*, 271.

participated in the Indiana Constitutional Convention of 1816 and served six terms in the General Assembly.[65]

Holman apparently found some time to spend at home because he fathered twelve children. Solomon, one of his sons, became an assistant engineer on the Wabash & Erie Canal. In 1823, Joseph Holman went to Fort Wayne as a political appointee by President Monroe. Holman served in the influential position as the first receiver of the land office established there. He was responsible for the disbursement of Indian annuities. He served in that capacity until 1829, when Andrew Jackson was elected, and he lost his political post. During this time, he accumulated real estate holdings and contacts within the business and political apparatus of the region that worked to his benefit. Following the Ewing family template of controlling business opportunities by becoming deeply involved in Fort Wayne politics, Holman also became the first county treasurer in Allen County in 1824. He was also a land commissioner alongside John Tipton and Alexander Ewing in 1825.[66] He then served on the Fort Wayne Board of Trustees with William Hood.[67] By serving in these capacities, Holman gained influence and made important contacts in the business community. He used those contacts wisely. The 1887 history of Peru also states that Holman "traded extensively in lands and all kinds of real estate ..."[68] Holman was successful at amassing a small fortune that gave him economic capital to expend as business opportunities became available.

Hood and Holman took similar routes to prominence in Fort Wayne by maneuvering themselves into positions that allowed them to promote their own interests. The political and economic bases they built supported their efforts to exploit the changing economic landscape of the upper Wabash Valley. By the late 1820s, Joseph Holman and

---

65 Blackford, *John Tipton Papers*, II, 228.
66 Griswold, *Pictorial History of Fort Wayne*, 273.
67 Ibid., 288.
68 Brant, *History of Miami County*, 435.

William Hood were both wealthy men. They were only waiting for the right opportunity to put that wealth to use. Whatever the reasons for their success, Joseph Holman, William Hood, and the various members of the Ewing family found themselves in an ideal position to capitalize on the changing landscape of the upper Wabash Valley.

Opportunity presented itself in the form of the Wabash & Erie Canal, Indiana's version of a gold rush. Historian Elliot West wrote of the far western frontier: "Waves of new experience rolled … into the continental center and as they did they set loose changes that surpassed in speed and scope anything the region had known."[69] That is also a perfect description of the change occurring along the Wabash River corridor by the late 1820s. Businessmen, engineers, and the fledgling US government saw the land in a new light, a reimagining that West called "the perceiving of the country as a fundamentally different realm of human use."[70]

In the case of the Wabash River, the process of reimagining began in earnest on March 2, 1827, when the federal government gave Indiana a land grant of 527,271 acres along the Wabash River for the intended purpose of financing a new canal along its path. Much of this was the Paradise Treaty land negotiated for just the previous October. The land grant was divided into alternating five section-wide segments along each side of the proposed route of the canal.[71] The grant stipulated that the canal be commenced within five years, completed in twenty, and that it be toll free for use by the federal government. The hope was that the sale of this land by Indiana would finance the construction of the canal and raise the surrounding land values, a further stimulus to see that the canal was completed, and that the federal government would recoup its

---

69   West, *Contested Plains*, xxii.
70   Ibid.
71   Harry N. Scheiber, "State Policy and the Public Domain: The Ohio Canal Lands," *Journal of Economic History* 25, no. 1 (1965): 88.

investment through land development.[72] The land was divided by the Americans into neatly partitioned parcels that resembled a chessboard where land speculators could place wagers. The Wabash River became a pawn in the new economic landscape.

Fort Wayne was ground zero for many of the speculators and canal supporters. Joseph Holman and William Hood stood with their feet firmly planted in both camps. By the time the Wabash & Erie Canal became a distinct possibility in 1827, both men had amassed great wealth in their dealings with the Indians, both held influential positions in the local government, and both had powerful friends. They were in an excellent position to capitalize on what they saw as the virgin territory along the Wabash River. The two men were well acquainted, and at least one account of Peru's history claims they were good friends.[73]

In 1827, there was virtually no white presence along the river between Fort Wayne and Lafayette. The river towns of the upper Wabash Valley were all settled after the canal was announced. Huntington saw its first settlers in 1830, Wabash and Peru in 1834, Miamisport (the predecessor of Peru) in 1829, Logansport in 1828, and Delphi in 1835. The prospect for growth between Fort Wayne, where the canal would tie into Lake Erie via the Maumee River, and Lafayette, where the Wabash became deep enough for shipping, was enormous. Those men who moved swiftly to acquire the best real estate along the proposed canal route were likely to make a killing.

Holman was the first one to try his luck, purchasing 640 acres a little less than two miles below the mouth of the Mississinewa River from Chief Richardville on August 18, 1827 for the sum of $500.[74] The section he purchased was one of the tracts given to Richardville in the Paradise Springs treaty just ten months before. Besides the prospect

---

72   John Bell Rae, "Federal Land Grants in Aid of Canals," *Journal of Economic History* 4, no. 2 (1944): 168.

73   Bodurtha, *History of Miami County*, 157.

74   Brant, *History of Miami County*, 362.

of the canal along the Wabash River, there were state plans to build another canal from Indianapolis to the mouth of the Mississinewa River, where it would connect with the Wabash and Erie Canal. This prospect made Holman's site especially valuable. Supposedly, Holman didn't pay the entire amount in cash, but "a thrifty trade was worked" in which Richardville received goods as part of the deal, a point noted with pride in every early written history of Peru.[75] This speaks both to the business acumen of Holman as well as his ethics. He planned a new town named Miamisport on the site.

Holman also purchased another section of land from Richardville near the mouth of the Eel River, paying $500 for that tract also.[76] The president had to approve the deal as part of a safety measure to prevent Indians from being cheated out of their land, but the system was corrupt because it relied on the judgment of local Indian agents to decide if the purchase price was fair. In this case, President John Quincy Adams dealt with John Tipton, who recommended approval, which the president gave on March 3, 1828.[77] Holman immediately sold the Eel River section to General Tipton for $600.[78] Tipton was working hard to get the Indian Agency moved to the new town of Logansport at that time and wanted to gain control of the Miami reserves that remained in the area.[79] Tipton and Holman were later accused by the competition of defrauding both Richardville and the federal government in this transaction, and the selling price of only $100 more than Holman originally paid does lend some credence to the idea of some kind of collusion between the two men, but nothing was ever proven. The charges were eventually dropped by the government after it decided they were politically motivated.

Joseph Holman was anxious to get the town of Miamisport platted

---

75   Stephens, *History of Miami County*, 174.
76   Blackford, *John Tipton Papers*, II, 24.
77   Bodurtha, *History of Miami County*, 153.
78   Blackford, *John Tipton Papers*, II, 24.
79   Charles R. Poinsatte, *Fort Wayne during the Canal Era: 1828–1855* (Indianapolis: Indiana Historical Bureau, 1969), 18.

on his new site along the Wabash River. On March 12, 1829, Holman hired a surveyor, who platted the town in the southwest corner of Holman's land. He included a public square and room for a marketplace. The south side of the new town bordered the Wabash River. Holman wanted to take advantage of the canal to make Miamisport a trade center.[80] He also hoped the new town would be a new county seat. At the time, the area of Miamisport was located within Cass County, which, at the time, incorporated much of northern Indiana. In anticipation of an influx of settlers when the canal became operational, the state planned to incorporate some new counties. In line with his perception of the land, Holman divided it into neat little parcels, drawing lines that gave him control of future economic development of the site. He built a log cabin along the river but soon moved into a fine stone house on higher ground between what is now Third and Main Streets.

Holman was not the only businessman interested in the area that was soon to be designated as Miami County. William Hood also played an integral part in the economic changes taking place along the Wabash. John H. Stephens's history of Peru states that Hood was among the first men to make Miamisport their home and lists Holman and Hood both as "the proprietors."[81] While the other two histories of the county do not list Hood as one of the town fathers, they do acknowledge that he was among the first men to come to Miamisport. The exact nature of his relationship with Joseph Holman is unknown, but the two men were at the very least well acquainted, and at most, friends. The truth probably lies somewhere in between. The two men were at different ends of the political spectrum, and Hood was part of the political faction that accused General Tipton, Holman's friend, of graft at one point, but they frequented the same business circles at Fort Wayne and shared a common background, so it is not unrealistic to think that the two men shared a business relationship. The ensuing conflict between

80   Bodurtha, *History of Miami County*, 153–54.
81   Stephens, *History of Miami County*, 177.

the two men exemplifies the new landscape that was taking shape as the perception of the Wabash River shifted from the traditional Native American view to that of the new American owners.

The value of the land was now based on its potential as a commodity, not on its value as a homesite or as a source of food. The economic potential of the Wabash & Erie Canal made the land Holman bought nothing more than a prospective source of revenue no different than a bar of gold or a canoe full of furs. On January 7, 1829, Joseph Holman sold William Hood 210 of the 640 acres along the Wabash River that he had purchased just four months before.[82] There is no record of why this transaction occurred, but in hindsight it seems that Holman displayed a horrendous lack of judgment. If Miamisport was the henhouse, Holman had just opened the door for a fox named Hood. The sale is a perfect example of the land speculation that was rampant at the time. Holman got $500 for the 210 acres. That was a 100 percent profit in less than five months, and Holman still had two-thirds of his land. Writing of this deal, historian Frank Fetter estimated that by 1887, the value of the original section bought by Holman had increased to $1,500,000. Fetter marked the sale to Hood as the beginning of the real estate boom in the area.[83] It also marked a rapid, permanent shift in the perceived patterns of power and wealth along the path of the proposed canal. Land equaled gold, and as Elliot West said about savvy businessmen taking advantage of the Colorado gold rush: "Some ... rode the changes to success while the others slipped into the cultural gloom."[84] That's exactly what happened to Joseph Holman and William Hood.

Hood made no immediate moves with his purchase, and over the next three years Miamisport slowly grew as traders and shopkeepers arrived and settled in to wait for the canal, while Hood's property to the east remained undeveloped. On February 2, 1832, the state

---

82   Bodurtha, *History of Miami County*, 153.
83   Brant, *History of Miami County*, 362.
84   West, *Contested Plains*, 190.

legislature passed an act creating Huntington, Wabash, and Miami Counties. The state did this in anticipation of the construction of the Wabash & Erie Canal and the flood of settlers it would bring to the upper Wabash Valley.[85] The construction of the Wabash & Erie Canal began with groundbreaking ceremonies in Fort Wayne on Washington's birthday, February 22, 1832. A talented man named Jesse Williams was appointed chief civil engineer for the project, and canal building began in earnest. This played into the hands of Joseph Holman, who wanted Miamisport to be named a county seat, guaranteeing financial success for the fledgling community as well as his investments.

The legislation that created Huntington, Wabash, and Miami Counties neglected to set up any specific apparatus for establishing county seats. By 1834, Indiana had appointed a set of commissioners to decide the matter. Joseph Holman groomed Miamisport for this honor, but he underestimated the will of William Hood. Hood had not done much with his 210 acres just east of Miamisport, but by 1834 the prospect of the canal was a reality, and Hood decided to lay out a town. He was prompted to move ahead when Holman made an effort to expand Miamisport to the west, enhancing his claim for a county seat. Hood quickly hired Stearns Fisher, an engineer employed on the canal, to lay out a new town on his 210 acres.[86] Holman was understandably angry at Hood, but it is surprising that he didn't anticipate the move. Whatever relationship had existed between the two men quickly dissolved into a bitter feud. "Violent words passed between them on several occasions and the quarrel became a matter of comment for the entire population."[87] The argument between the two men failed to stop Hood, and he pushed ahead with the platting of his own town. The work was done quickly, and by the time the commissioners met in June 1834, Hood and Holman were prepared for a showdown.

---

85   Bodurtha, *History of Miami County*, 96.
86   Ibid., 157.
87   Ibid.

On the surface, it appeared that Holman had the superior position. Miamisport was already five years old, and, even though it was small, there were a number of businesses established there along with a few settlers. All Hood owned was an unimproved tract of land and a piece of paper showing an unbuilt town. According to a contemporary account, the land was in fact a mess: "the site was entirely covered with heavy timber and a thick, impenetrable growth of underbrush. Not a rod square was cleared."[88] Fisher, the engineer, had to send men out in front of him to clear away the brush so he could get a sight through his surveying transit. He didn't even have a name for the town. When Hood was pressed about a name, his only answer was that he didn't care as long as it was "something short."[89] After some discussion, a few of Hood's associates chose the name Peru, an Indian word meaning "straight place in the river." It was not an auspicious start.

Under ordinary circumstances, it seems the choice for the new county seat was a simple one, but 1834 was not a simple time on the Wabash River, and William Hood and Joseph Holman were not ordinary men. Miamisport was a real town while Peru was only lines on a piece of paper, but when the state commissioners made their decision in June 1834, they chose the unbuilt city of Peru as the seat of Miami County. In this case, lines on a piece of paper were a more potent argument for creating a new landscape than was an existing town.

How did William Hood succeed in the face of such long odds? The 1914 history of Peru at first puts it delicately, saying that "Mr. Hood was something of a diplomat." Later in the same paragraph, the account states the truth bluntly: "Money talks was certainly true in this instance."[90] Hood had merely done what everyone else did along the upper Wabash Valley: he finagled the county seat by peddling favors and influence.

---

88   Brant, *History of Miami County*, 363.

89   Stephens, *History of Miami County*, 179.

90   Bodurtha, *History of Miami County*, 157.

When Hood made his pitch to the commissioners, he executed a bond stipulating that if Peru was chosen by the state for the county seat, he would do a number of things. He promised to donate the land for a public square as well as the money to build a courthouse and a jail. He also promised to donate a prime city lot to each of the major religious denominations for the purpose of building churches. In addition, he promised $125 for the establishment of a town library. Hood also went to the merchants in Miamisport and promised them either free lots in the new town or ones at subsidized rates for their homes and businesses. Some of the best lots went for $50. Lastly, Hood approached two very influential men, Richard L. Britton and Jesse L. Williams, and sold both of them a one-third interest in his new town for $3,000 each.[91] Britton was an influential businessman, and Williams was the chief civil engineer in charge of constructing the Wabash & Erie Canal.

In one fell swoop, William Hood gained the support of the state of Indiana (free courthouse and jail), religious leaders (free land for churches), local businessmen (free or cheap lots), the financial backing of a rich businessman (Britton), and the cooperation of the man who would decide the path of the new canal (Williams). Even though there is evidence that Hood reneged on some of his promises, he won the battle between Miamisport and Peru.

While doing this, he sold two-thirds of his original $500 investment for $6,000 and dramatically increased the value of the one-third he still owned. Hood single-handedly changed the perception and value of his property without building anything. It was a stroke of genius. The imagined town of Peru quickly became a reality. Joseph Holman soon sold his interest in Miamisport and left Miami County for good. His town withered on the vine and was eventually annexed by Peru in 1841.

Peru, the "straight place on the river," came into existence during

---

91   Brant, *History of Miami County*, 364.

the greatest time of change the Wabash River Valley ever saw. Shifting ideas about land, water, and the wealth that could be extracted from them were encapsulated in historical events leading to the founding of Peru. The Miami, Potawatomi, and the other Indian tribes who saw water as the source of spiritual life and daily labor and sustenance treated the Wabash River with respect, but the Americans who gained dominance over the area by 1834 saw the Wabash in a different light.

Peru was born because of the river, but men like Joseph Holman and William Hood didn't see the Wabash as the source of spiritual life for the new town. To them the river became a commodity and the power of the water an economic bargaining chip to be used as a way to equate the landscape with a gold rush. The river was merely a catalyst for a new economic landscape, one dictated not by the natural rhythm of the land and the water, but by man-made rules of business and finance. Hood and Holman literally imagined Peru into existence with a liberal application of wealth and influence. They anticipated the construction of a transportation and trading center that would depend on the Wabash & Erie Canal for its economic growth.

As a consequence, a new cultural landscape evolved—one in which the Wabash River was no longer in the foreground. Over the next eighty years, the perception of the river continued to change in the eyes of the people of Peru. At first, the Wabash was an ally in the growth of the town. After the decline of the canal, it became a nuisance. Eventually it became an enemy as the economic fortunes of the town fell because the river refused to behave.

CHAPTER 2

How the Wabash & Erie Canal Reshaped the Landscape

THE NEW LANDSCAPE EMERGING ALONG THE WABASH RIVER BY 1834 was not the one envisioned by the first Americans who settled in the region. Peru grew rapidly but not exactly in the way people anticipated. The first surge of economic growth for the new city began with the construction of the Wabash and Erie Canal and the massive influx of immigrants along the upper Wabash Valley that accompanied it. The decision to build a feeder dam for the canal in Peru had long-lasting consequences to the economic and social fabric of the town. The canal also brought a massive influx of immigrants to the region, which was responsible for social and environmental changes to the area. Those changes showed that the relationship between the human and nonhuman world were far more complicated and unpredictable than anyone expected.

Even before Peru was designated as the county seat in June 1834, an announcement appeared in the *Logansport Canal Telegraph* calling for canal workers in the area. Workers were offered three to four years of work along with an opportunity to become landowners along the canal "through hard work."[92] Laborers gravitated to the area, drawn by the promise of an economic boom. Peru was, as yet, nothing more than an idea covered in a dense tangle of oak, maple, and other hardwoods. The sound of axes and saws soon echoed through the forest, and the smoke from dozens of brush fires wafted over the Wabash as men transformed the virgin forest into a new frontier town. Hood's vision moved rapidly from idea to reality as men cleared lots, converted timber into cabins, and cut arrow-straight paths through the forest to delineate new streets.

Most of the initial work concentrated on the land near the Wabash River where the canal would soon be. When William Hood, Richard Britton, and Jesse Williams held the first land sale at Miamisport on July 26, 1834, the waterfront lots along Canal Street sold first and brought the highest prices. Exact prices are impossible to ascertain because of an 1843 fire that destroyed most of the early land records, but the historical testimony verifies that it was a raucous, busy, and profitable day for the land speculators.[93] The owners of Peru also signed the first contracts for canal construction through Miami County on that day, guaranteeing an influx of workers and the prospect of lucrative local contracts for building materials. Daniel Bearss and Alphonso Cole, two of the businessmen who would anchor the economic progress of downtown Peru, arrived at this time.[94] They were, however, not the most important figure of that day. That honor fell to the man responsible for construction of the new canal.

Jesse L. Williams was the member of the land ownership triumvirate most responsible for the pivotal event in the industrial development of Peru.

---

92   *Logansport Canal Telegraph,* April 12, 1834.
93   Bodurtha, *History of Miami County,* 158.
94   Ibid.

Jesse Williams, chief engineer for the Wabash & Erie Canal
(Photo courtesy of the Miami County, Indiana, Historical Society)

As chief engineer of the Wabash and Erie Canal, it was his responsibility to decide the exact location for the construction of a feeder dam across the Wabash River along the Miami County portion of the canal.[95] The dam was necessary to provide a reliable source of water for the canal. It would also generate the hydraulic power needed for economic development. Williams chose a spot about a quarter mile below the mouth of the Mississinewa River. This choice gave the fledgling town of Peru the superior economic position over Miamisport because of the easy availability of water power from the new dam.[96] The choice was somewhat of a surprise because a more favorable spot seemed to be farther downriver, where the bottom was not as sandy. A dam there would have been cheaper to build. However, Williams just happened to be the owner of a third of the land in Peru and had an economic

---

95   Charles B. Stuart, *Lives and Works of Civil and Military Engineers of America* (New York: D. Van Nostrand, 1871), 146.

96   Brant and Fuller, eds., *History of Miami County Indiana* (Chicago: Brant and Fuller, 1887), 364.

stake in the new town. He also just happened to own the parcel of land where the suggested dam site was. He made his choice accordingly. For Miamisport, "hopes of greatness departed."[97] Joseph Holman promptly accused Williams of corruption, and in 1836 he presented his accusation to a select committee established by the Indiana House of Representatives. Holman accused the engineer of choosing the site of the feeder dam to "destroy the town of Miamisport for the purpose of building up and increasing the value of the town of Peru."[98]

The charge seemed obvious, but the line between guilt and innocence was rather blurry along the frontier. Dam sites on the proposed canal were influential for economic and political reasons. Engineers such as Williams were quick to recognize the clout the dams would have in the decision process for the location of new towns and industries, giving the engineers' decisions an inordinate amount of weight. It was not uncommon for land speculators to become involved in private ventures with the engineers of various canal projects in the hopes of influencing the location of important infrastructure.[99] While his actions may have been questionable by today's ethical standards, in 1834 it was acceptable practice, and the House of Representatives found Williams innocent.[100]

The location of Feeder Dam Number Three at the eastern fringe of Peru had far-reaching implications on early industrial development and capital growth in the area. The location was ideal; cheap water power and convenient access to the new canal made the site almost perfect. As a result, the first industries chose sites near the feeder dam because of the water power it provided.

---

97   Ibid.
98   Indiana House of Representatives, "Select Committee of the House of Representatives in the Case of Jesse L. Williams, Principal Engineer, January 4, 1836," *Documentary Journal* (1836).
99   Harry N. Scheiber, "Entrepreneurship and Western Development: The Case of Micajah T. Williams," *Business History Review* 37.4 (Winter 1963), 354.
100   Indiana House of Representatives. *Documentary Journal* (1836).

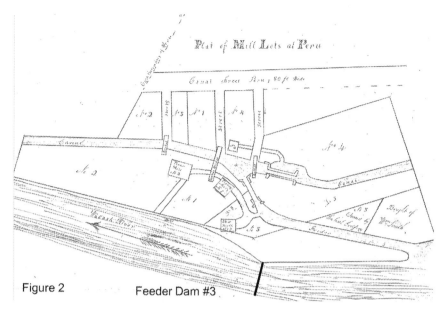

Figure 2   Feeder Dam #3

Map of the feeder dam at the eastern edge of Peru
(Photo courtesy of the Miami County, Indiana, Historical Society)

A local newspaper advertised the availability of "a valuable mill site" for lease well before the canal reached Peru.[101] The canal authority accepted sealed bids, and a sawmill, planing mill, flouring mill, and one unidentified mill were built by entrepreneurs at the site.[102]

If land speculation marked the first economic surge in Peru, the construction of the mills introduced the second wave of infusion of capital as businesses flocked to the area. They provided construction materials for the canal and saw to the everyday needs of the laborers digging it. Peru was rich in timber that was needed to make the lumber for the building of locks, dams, bridges, and aqueducts along the canal. Mills and livery stables fed and shod the horses and mules dredging the canal.

Most importantly, a large number of canal workers quickly increased the population of Peru. Business needed to address the requirements of

101   *Logansport Canal Telegraph*, April 12, 1834.
102   "Plat of Mill Lots at Peru," Miami County Recorder, 1851. Book 1, 584.

a growing populace. A visitor to Peru in early 1835 commented that it was already a small village of "one to two hundred inhabitants, many of whom were laborers on the canal."[103] Another contemporary visitor said the village was "filled with people working on the Wabash & Erie Canal from different states."[104] The number of workers and immigrants grew quickly, and they needed food to eat, liquor to drink, clothes to wear, and tools to ply their trade. A "wild and rough" group of merchants swarmed to Peru and set up shop along Canal Street, Second Street, and Broadway.[105] They wanted to be in on the economic ground floor as the canal inched toward the town.

An important economic and environmental corollary to the manufacturing geography of the new town stemmed from the fact that the industrial center was so close to the mouth of the Mississinewa River. While practical at the time, it highlights the misperception the pioneers had about their relationship with the river. Nineteenth century American ideas about cultural superiority, or Manifest Destiny, contributed to a collective conviction that nature existed to be conquered, not accommodated. John O'Sullivan said in 1839: "We are the nation of human progress, and who will, what can, set limits to our onward march? Providence is with us, and no earthly power can."[106] The "onward march" inspired people to gobble up land voraciously because "land represented wealth and progress to the average American," who saw the frontier as an untapped source of riches.[107] They didn't consider what the true cost of those riches might be.

The man who built dam Number Three on the Wabash & Erie

---

103 Brant, *History of Miami County*, 364.
104 Ibid.
105 Ibid., 365.
106 John O'Sullivan, "The Great Nation of Futurity," *The United States Democratic Review* 6 (no. 23), 427.
107 J. T. Moriarty, *Manifest Destiny: A Primary Source History of America's Territorial Expansion in the 19th Century* (New York: Rosen Publishing, 2005), 5.

Canal at Peru is a perfect example of this vision of national destiny implemented on a local scale. Jesse L. Williams was an extraordinary engineer who not only built the largest canal in the western hemisphere but also went on to help build the transcontinental railroad. He was an expert in nineteenth century engineering techniques.[108] He knew his craft. The dam he built at Peru was four hundred feet long, one hundred feet wide, and eleven feet tall, and was constructed out of brush, trees, and stone. He reported that the dam was "a safe and permanent structure."[109] His engineering expertise reflected the conventional view that man could divert and control nature. He foresaw the possibility of floods, but was confident that his engineering skills could compensate for natural disasters. His assessment of the dam was correct only as long as workers performed constant maintenance. The "permanence" of the dam was constantly under assault by the river. Floods, ice flows, and debris sought a way around or through the structure.[110] It remained in place until the canal was abandoned and fell into disrepair. Part of it finally washed out in 1876, and the rest was removed a few years later. In 1942, a contractor hired to dredge the river stumbled across the foundation of the dam. He said, "Whoever built that dam was an engineering genius and it was certainly a remarkable piece of work."[111] Traces of the dam can still be seen on the south side of the river just above the Wayne Street Bridge when the water is low. Only a few timbers remain.

Yes, Williams knew how to build a dam, but his vision of human control was limited by his understanding of the place of his dam within

---

108 Stuart, *Lives and Works,*152.

109 Jesse L. Williams, *Wabash & Erie Canal 1847 Chief Engineers Report on Structures, 1847.*

110 Thomas E. Castaldi, *Wabash & Erie Canal Notebook III: Wabash and Miami Counties* (Fort Wayne, IN: Parrot Printing, 2004), 124.

111 Carolyn I. Schmidt, ed., *Wabash & Erie Canal in Miami County and in Portions of Wabash and Cass Counties* (Fort Wayne: Canal Society of Indiana, 2000), 45.

the natural landscape. He saw the structure as separate from nature and failed to fully appreciate the consequences of building it so close to the mouth of the Mississinewa River. He didn't fully understand or appreciate that there are consequences when people constantly alter their environment—digging, moving, and rearranging the land and water. Whether subtly or overtly, nature always reacts to those changes.

The new residents along the Wabash River failed to recognize that interaction between what is man-made and what is not blurs the environmental line in unanticipated ways. The contact is a continuous give-and-take that results in "a process of alteration, intermingling, and layering, the result of which is landscape."[112] In the case of Peru, the landscape created by Feeder Dam Number Three caused the economic epicenter of the town to gravitate to a seemingly advantageous commercial location when, in fact, the manufacturing center and the business district of Peru were built in the worst possible location imaginable. The Wabash River was aimed at the town of Peru like a shotgun, with the mouth of the Mississinewa River serving as the trigger. No one in the 1830s understood the scope of what would happen when the Wabash and Mississinewa went over, around, and through the town. While the new residents of the area appreciated the economic advantages of the river, they failed to discern the environmental intricacies of the new urban landscape they were creating.

In contrast, while the Miami Indians were confused by the economic reality of the new landscape, they knew the nature of the river intimately. One story in particular illuminates the different relationship the Indians had with the landscape. When the construction of the canal reached the Indian village of White Raccoon, in what is now Huntington County, it became apparent that the cabin of the tribe's orator and chief, Cha-pine, was in the way of the canal bed and needed to be moved. According to one of the engineers surveying the site, Cha-pine was not thrilled

---

112   Mark Fiege, *Irrigated Eden: The Making of an Agricultural Landscape in the American West* (Seattle: University of Washington Press, 1999), 9.

at the prospect of having his home relocated. When he saw the canal engineers driving stakes in the ground, he asked what they signified. The engineers tried to explain about the canal, telling Cha-pine that the white man was bringing a new river to the land. The Miami chief took on a look of contempt and said, "Can't do it; won't rain enough to fill it; white man a fool; the Great Spirit made the rivers."[113] Cha-pine was not an engineer, but he understood that the river could not be remade that easily. Nature cannot be negated by economics and survey stakes.

The people of Peru learned this lesson the hard way. The lesson began on the day the Wabash & Erie Canal reached Peru, the Fourth of July, 1837. By then, the population was between five and seven hundred and the town had almost a hundred buildings. Many of the citizens were itinerant canal workers, but the number of people making Peru a permanent home increased each day. News of the impending arrival of the packet boat *Indiana* caused quite a commotion. The town fathers planned a public ceremony to welcome the crew and passengers of the first canal boat to reach Peru, and virtually everyone in town gathered to celebrate the momentous occasion. The town's first newspaper, the *Peru Forester*, chronicled the events of the day. By noon "the town was filled with people of the county, to witness the grand display on the occasion."[114] The gathering was anticlimactic. After a long wait, word came that the boat had grounded at the lock by the feeder dam. The banks of the new canal had not had time to settle and were absorbing more water than anticipated. Cha-pine's prediction was already holding more water than the canal, but no one saw it as anything other than a temporary setback. Not to be deterred, the townsfolk walked or rode the mile to the lock and escorted the crew and passengers back to the National Hotel at the corner of Miami and Canal Streets, where they were entertained by music and dancing.[115] The *Indiana* then returned

---

113   Stuart, *Lives and Works*, 145.
114   Bodurtha, *History of Miami County*, 247.
115   Ibid., 248.

to Fort Wayne. A few days later, after the canal was able to hold water, it returned and was able to dock in downtown Peru, signaling the functional opening of the canal.

By 1837, the economic boom gained momentum. Up until the first canal boat docked, Peru's economy was geared almost solely toward the building of the canal. Local businessmen already profited from the canal workers. Those laborers averaged sixty cents a day in wages. They spent much of that money on food, clothing, and alcohol at local business establishments. The lumber yards and flour mills churned out products that went almost exclusively to canal contractors. By the middle of July, and despite the fact that the canal opened in the midst of the Panic of 1837, cheap manufactured goods from the East finally became available to the people of Miami County.

As early as two weeks after the first boat arrived in Peru, advertisements in the *Peru Forester* offered merchandise "just received from New York, via the canal" to the citizens of Peru and the surrounding area. The proprietor of the store, Jacob Linzee, also pointed out that "most kinds of country produce and peltries [would be] taken in exchange for goods."[116] Mr. Linzee realized that his economic future was not defined solely by the boundaries of the new town. The opening of the canal also gave outlying farms access to the economic boom.

The opening of the Wabash & Erie Canal quickly integrated the economy of Peru with that of the eastern United States. Goods could not only flow in; there was now a cheap, efficient way to transport local agricultural products back East. Shipping rates quickly plunged from around fifteen cents a ton-mile for cargo shipped by wagon over primitive roads to rates of one to two cents a ton-mile on the canal, which was also much quicker and more efficient.[117] Farmers along the

---

116   *Peru Forester*, July 26, 1837.
117   David R. Meyer, "Midwestern Industrialization and the American Manufacturing Belt in the Nineteenth Century," *Journal of Economic History* 49.4 (1989): 927.

upper Wabash Valley increased in number, cleared more land, and bought modern tools shipped in on the canal. When construction of the canal started in 1832, only about twelve thousand people were in the region. By 1840, that number grew to 270,000.[118] Canal boats that carried grain up the canal to Lake Erie returned with settlers from the East. Rural land sales in Miami County grew exponentially as more people came to farm the land. Between 1840 and 1850, the population of the counties along the canal grew over 400 percent, more than twice the average for the rest of Indiana. By 1844, four hundred wagonloads a day waited to unload the harvest at towns along the canal.[119] Peru was smack in the middle of this economic and cultural landslide.

Canal boosters and land speculators who preached the gospel of urban expansion inherent in the internal improvement movement that led to the digging of the canal saw validation in the growth of towns such as Peru. It was a testimony to Manifest Destiny. The population of Peru almost tripled during the same time period, reaching 1,266 by 1850, almost as big as Fort Wayne.[120] Peru expanded steadily after the canal opened in 1837, with the tax base quadrupling between 1841 and 1850.[121] Industry and general business concentrated along a waterfront that stretched approximately one and one-half miles along the river from the feeder dam to a point a few blocks west of Broadway. Canal Street in particular was a hive of activity by the early 1840s. "The thoroughfare was a locale for stores, inns, and whiskey shops, a center of sociability, a likely place for fights, and a roadway for wagonload after wagonload of valley grain rumbling down it to canal warehouses."[122]

Evolving perception of the landscape embraced more than the

---

118   Bodurtha, *History of Miami County*, 248.
119   Ibid., 249.
120   Brant, *History of Miami County*, 371.
121   John H. Stephens, *History of Miami County: Illustrated* (Peru, IN: John H. Stephens Publishing, 1896), 93.
122   Paul Fatout, *Indiana Canals* (West Lafayette, IN: Purdue University Press, 1972), 134.

economic signs of success. The trappings of modern civilization slowly made their way to Peru. One could eat at the Buck Tavern, so named for the hunting trophies that graced its walls. Venison was on the menu, but one customer recalled the average meal as consisting of "hard bread, stale butter, with an old potato and an egg, sometimes rotten."[123] The first elected city government was organized in 1842; apparently, the biggest problem they dealt with was preventing hogs from running loose in the streets. "Ordinance after ordinance was framed, but there always seemed a crack through which a pig could crawl."[124] Civilization had reached Peru.

Canal Street was the economic heart of the town. Corduroy roads that stretched from Peru to the small rural towns springing up in the county radiated out from Peru like the spokes on a wheel. Each day, new homesteaders arrived at the docks, and each day more farmers cleared ground. In turn, more crops made their way to the mills and warehouses along Canal Street, where they were shipped east to New York or south to New Orleans after the canal reached Lafayette. It was a perfect example of "a symbiotic relationship between cities and their surrounding countrysides."[125] In Peru's case, this relationship was totally dependent on the Wabash and Erie Canal. But as the town grew, so did the tendency to forget the source of the canal's power.

The more organized Peru became, the more the new owners of the land saw a separation between nature and themselves. As building after building went up along the canal, the less people could see of the river. The canal not only separated the river from the town, it seemed to separate what was man-made from what was natural. By 1848, newspaper accounts in Peru mentioned shipping rates, manifests, and canal problems on a daily basis but rarely mentioned the river. To the

---

123 Brant, *History of Miami County*, 367.
124 Ibid.
125 William Cronon, *Nature's Metropolis: Chicago and the Great West* (New York: W. W. Norton, 1991), 34.

people of Peru, the river and the canal were separate entities, reinforcing the notion that "we do not normally interpret heavily used landscapes, places of work and production, as environments that are also natural."[126] The canal and its attendant waterfront were literally and figuratively above the river in the minds of Peruvians.

When the canal began to experience unexpected economic difficulties attributable to intrusions by nature, people were forced to rethink the relationship between the river and the town, learning that "when humans disturb the environment, they almost invariably make it better for certain flora and fauna; destruction and creation go hand in hand."[127] The Wabash was no different. People who lived along the river were always aware of the power flowing down the Wabash; it's why they came to its banks. They had a working knowledge of the river because of their daily contact with it, a view explained by historian Richard White. Speaking of the Columbia River, he suggested that "the river was felt in human bones and sinews; humans knew the river through the work the river demanded of them."[128] While that was the traditional way of knowing a river, by the mid-1840s the new occupants of the Upper Wabash River Valley saw their relationship with the river in a different light because of the canal.

Americans saw a new landscape, one shaped by economic development, not the natural ebb and flow of the environment. The Americans wanted to know the river not by the work it demanded of them, but by demanding that the river work for them. The Wabash & Erie Canal was the physical embodiment of the new economic philosophy. The canal harnessed the power of the river and converted it into an economic asset that could be controlled at will by opening a

---

126 Fiege, *Irrigated Eden*, 9.
127 Tim Palmer, *The Snake River: Window to the West* (Washington, DC: Island Press, 1991), 185.
128 Richard White, *The Organic Machine: The Remaking of the Columbia River* (New York: Hill and Wang, 1995), 4.

valve or closing a lock. Water became a commodity to be bought and sold. An 1844 ad placed by the canal authority in the *Miami County Sentinel* asked for sealed bids for the right to put a waterwheel at one of the new canal locks east of Peru. The lessee would be entitled to "the use of all water that flows over the tumble" with the proviso that no deduction in rent would be made "in consequence of a deficiency of water."[129] They could sell the water even if it wasn't there.

The canal was both a geographical and philosophical dividing line between the old perception of the landscape and the new. When that line was eroded by nature, it called into question the superiority of man's technology. At times, as in the ad just mentioned, lack of total control was simply ignored in the belief that human expertise would always find a way to succeed. The canal diverted water into a uniform channel forty feet wide and four feet deep and regulated it through a series of dams and locks to provide safe and economical transportation. From a purely technological point of view, it seemed like a workable process. In reality, the interaction between man and nature along the canal was less one-sided and far more complicated than anyone anticipated. Nature had not vanished; it merely asserted itself in different and unexpected ways.

Problems with the canal began even before it was finished. Engineers failed to take into account many of the ways nature would affect the canal.[130] For starters, it tended to leak (as evidenced by the failure of the *Indiana* to make it into Peru in 1837). The bottom of the canal was sandy in many places, requiring the use of "puddle," a waterproof material made from clay, to stop water absorption. Wooden aqueducts and culverts along the path of the canal tended to freeze and thaw during the winter, causing numerous leaks. Ice on the canal brought traffic to a halt for extended periods of time. The Wabash River flooded

129 *The Miami County Sentinel*, April 26, 1844.
130 Robert Wallace Ward, *The Wabash and Erie Canal: A Beautiful Dream* (Robert W. Ward, 1983), 9.

periodically, causing breaks in the canal walls that sometimes took months to fix. One flood in June 1858 caused so many breaks that the canal closed for the rest of the year.[131] In extreme cases, breaks in the canal caused fatalities. Because of the mistaken belief that water could be harnessed like one of the mules that pulled the canal boats, operation of the Wabash & Erie Canal was proving to be more complicated than anyone anticipated.

A July 13, 1844, article in the *Peru Observer* noted that water was back in the canal to Peru after a break but that navigation to Logansport would take a few days to restore. The repairs from Logansport to Lafayette were at least three weeks away from completion. A three-week blockage of canal traffic in July was devastating to the local economy.[132] In an editorial one week later, the *Observer* excoriated the local canal superintendent, accusing him of delaying repairs for political purposes. Over the next two weeks, the rhetoric increased as revenues declined. Every mention of this incident in the Peru newspapers laid the blame for the breakages on willful negligence, political chicanery, or incompetence. There was no mention of nature as an adversary to economic development. In the eyes of the people who depended on the canal, failure was due only to lack of foresight. "Many of the worst breaks ... might have been prevented ... had they been attended to in season."[133] Again, a few weeks later, the *Peru Observer* noted another breach near the town of Lagro that would take one hundred men a month to repair. In another story, in September 1844, the newspaper exasperatingly mentioned yet another break near Logansport. They couldn't explain it because "not a drop of rain had fallen to occasion it,"[134] as though rain was the only possible offender nature could produce.

During 1844, that story was the one single reference in the Peru

---

131 *The Peru Republican*, June 15, 1858.
132 Ibid., July 13, 1844.
133 Ibid.
134 *The Peru Observer*, September 29, 1844.

papers referring to tribulations on the canal that even hinted at the role the environment played in the problem. The frustrations evoked in the newspapers stemmed from the desire to answer a complicated problem with a simple solution when the problem was not merely man-made: it was man-made *and* natural.

This interaction continually played out along the Wabash and Erie Canal. The banks of the canal show how this connection developed. The banks separated what was man-made (the canal) from what was natural (the river), but the dividing line often disappeared when the banks were damaged. Some of the damage was self-inflicted by those who worked the canal. Horses and mules walking the towpath after a heavy rain would occasionally slip and fall into the waterway, causing damage to the banks. Canal boats ran into the banks, gouging the earth and damaging pilings. Crewmen used long poles to push their wayward craft back into the channel. The poles pushed deep into the banks and often led to leaks. Timber was one of the most common items shipped on the canal, and strings of logging rafts were a common sight. They sometimes broke loose, hitting banks, bridges, and aqueducts.[135] Dramatic cost overruns during construction, along with the financially disastrous Indiana internal improvement program, resulted in a lack of maintenance along the canal. Mills siphoned off more water than they contracted for, causing water levels to drop and leading to navigation problems. Passengers and crews of the canal boats denuded the land along the canal looking for firewood, which led to more erosion. While the canal undoubtedly suffered from a host of man-made problems, there were straightforward solutions for most of them. More problematic to the towns that depended on the canal were the troubles that were not self-inflicted.

The largest threat to the stability of the canal came from the natural factors the builders of the canal either underestimated or failed to

---

135 Ward, *Wabash and Erie Canal*, 18–20.

anticipate. Weather, vegetation, animals, and the river all played a role in breaching the canal. Winter travel on the canal was impossible. For up to five months out of the year, the canal was closed either because of ice or extremes in water levels. Freezing and thawing caused damage to viaducts, bridges, and the canal banks. Heavy rains could cause breaches and make the towpath unusable. It was not uncommon for boats to wash through these breaks into a farmer's field or into the river. After one heavy rain in June 1844, the packet boat *Kentucky* was swept through a breach between Peru and Logansport, drowning three people.[136] Salvage costs were high, and many of the boats were left to rot, at times becoming a new home for squatters.[137]

At other times, drought would cause the water level in the Wabash River to drop below the minimum level needed to maintain reservoirs that fed the canal. General upkeep of the canal was often scheduled for midsummer when the water level made it easier to replace locks and culverts. Summer was also better for maintenance because there was less seasonal economic pressure to keep the canal open. It was more important to keep the canal running in the spring, when most of the pork was shipped out, and in the fall, when the harvest meant large grain shipments.[138]

Vegetation and animals also caused unexpected problems along the canal. Invasive plants along the Wabash River have a tendency to take advantage of large swings in water depth. They can survive high water and spread vigorously in low water.[139] The canal bed offered a perfect platform for the proliferation of aquatic plants, and they soon became a serious problem. Cattails and other weeds made navigation difficult in places. Laborers faced a constant battle cutting water vegetation. Canal

---

136 *The Peru Observer*, June, 1844.

137 Ward, *Wabash and Erie Canal*, 21.

138 Schmidt, *Wabash & Erie Canal*, 60.

139 Alton A. Asdall, Robert O. Lindsey, David K. Sterling, Willard Van, "Vegetation and Environment Along the Wabash and Tippecanoe Rivers," *Ecological Monographs* 31.2 (1961): 111.

engineers even invented a special submarine mower that worked up and down the canal continuously, cutting weeds.[140] The weeds also made the canal a perfect breeding ground for fish. They soon filled the canal in large quantities. The fish then attracted animals such as raccoons, muskrats, otters, and beavers. These animals burrowed into the banks of the canal, causing more breaches and erosion.[141] A law that forbade fishing in the canal was soon abandoned as groundhogs, beaver, and other animals attracted by the prospect of a fish dinner turned portions of the canal into Swiss cheese. The people who depended on the canal began to see it in a different light, learning that "when humans disturb the environment, they almost invariably make it better for certain flora and fauna; destruction and creation go hand in hand."[142]

Human interference was also a source of problems along the canal, as well as a convenient explanation for some of the thornier questions arising about the relationship between humans and nature along the Wabash River. The water level of the canal was sometimes inconsistent, making travel unreliable even with the existence of dams and reservoirs. At times, boats were stranded for days on end while shippers and newspaper editorials waxed eloquent on the subjects of poor management, greedy mill owners who drew too much water, and incompetent repair crews.[143]

Since problems caused by human shortcomings were often easier to fix than the larger environmental ones, blame for canal woes was sometimes directed by critics in the wrong direction. One telling 1844 editorial in *The Peru Observer* blamed a four-week delay in opening the canal on "the negligence and indolence of those having charge of

---

140   James R. Gammon, *The Wabash River Ecosystem* (Bloomington: Indiana University Press, 1998), 16.
141   Ward, *Wabash and Erie Canal*, 17.
142   Tim Palmer, *The Snake River: Window to the West.* (Washington DC: Island Press, 1991), 185.
143   Fatout, *Indiana Canals*, 105.

it."[144] It also blamed nine out of ten local breaches on negligence by the local superintendent even while acknowledging that "the water had been eating away at the banks for weeks …"[145] It was far easier to blame flesh and bone for failure than it was to admit that humans had underestimated the place of the river in the new landscape they were trying to create.

America was in the midst of unprecedented advances in technology, and most people had confidence in "the power of engineers and inventors to overcome environmental obstacles."[146] Jesse Williams believed that with due care, the canal would stand against whatever troubles either humans or the river caused. In his 1847 "Chief Engineer's Report" to the state legislature, he constantly defined canal structures by their estimated lifespan. He used phrases such as "permanent for ten or fifteen years," "needs renewal in two years," and "will last one or two years longer" in his evaluation of some of the canal structures in and around Peru.[147] His appraisal of Lock Number Nineteen at the east end of Canal Street stated that although it was made from cut stone, it was "not durable, beginning to yield to the action of the weather. With some repairs, may last eight or ten years."[148]

Williams believed that the technology of the day would provide a barrier to the power of the Wabash and that constant maintenance could keep the canal operating efficiently. He was correct to a point, as early years of flooding along the river valley demonstrated. Although the river constantly breached its banks and damaged structures, Williams stayed on top of the problem and kept the canal functioning. However, while his engineering skills were strong, he overestimated the capacity of technology to maintain the line between man and the environment.

---

144 *The Peru Observer*, July, 1844.

145 Ibid.

146 Ari Kelman, *A River and Its City: The Nature of Landscape in New Orleans* (Berkeley: University of California Press, 2006), 134.

147 Schmidt, *Wabash & Erie Canal*, 13–15.

148 Ibid., 14.

Understanding a flood on the Wabash River was one thing; coping with the consequences of the human flood pouring into the Upper Wabash River Valley was another.

The Wabash & Erie Canal brought economic development to Peru but not environmental control. Once the canal was open, the influx of people into Miami County accelerated rapidly, resulting in a frontier way of life along the waterfront. Each day during the season, boats of all kinds passed back and forth through Peru, stopping to unload passengers and cargo, or picking up corn and wheat from the warehouses springing up along Canal Street. There were passenger packets; bateaus carrying trappers west; rough boats and rafts carrying immigrants; cargo boats full of nails, farm implements, and cloth; and factory boats loaded down with tons of potash or firewood. There were even entertainment boats with sides that folded out to make a stage. Canal historian Robert Wallace Ford called the activities along the canal waterfronts "pure pandemonium," pointing out that the canal even supported floating bordellos with women whose appearance on deck "brought more catcalls, whistles, and 'goldangs!' from the men on shore than any wrestling match would ever warrant."[149]

The general perception of the waterfront changed over time and with economic growth. In 1837, the town populace marched joyfully down to the feeder dam to welcome the first canal boat and the prosperity it symbolized. By the mid-1840s, as the canal was nearing its peak, people began to understand that the canal brought more than prosperity to Peru; it also brought crime and disease.

Crime came in many forms, but most were linked to the economic development of the area. Land speculation remained rampant in Miami County. In 1844, there was still more profit to be made buying and selling land than in farming it.[150] The canal land office was located in

---

149 Ward, *Wabash and Erie Canal*, 16.
150 Harvey L. Carter, "Rural Indiana in Transition, 1850–1860," *Agricultural History* 20.2 (1946): 108.

Peru, and the town became a magnet for speculators and swindlers. Two men named Morris and Fitzgerald pushed a dubious bill through the state legislature in 1846 that declared all canal lands with delinquent taxes to be forfeited to the highest bidder. The two men rushed to the land office in Peru as soon as the governor signed the bill. There, in cooperation with the clerk, they locked themselves in, and the two men began going through the records picking and choosing which plots of land to grab. Word leaked out, and when a large, angry crowd gathered to see what was going on, the two men beat a hasty retreat. Indiana soon repealed the law.[151]

Much of the crime centered on the canal itself. The crews on the canal boats were a tough bunch. They cussed, drank, fought, and generally raised hell as they went up and down the canal. Rivalries between boats led to fights along the towpath, many of which turned violent. According to canal historian Paul Fatout, "A chance encounter of boatmen and Irishmen usually meant a donnybrook of ... gouging and head-cracking ... woe betide the innocent bystander who did not run for cover."[152] On one occasion, the sheriff in Peru had to ride out toward Logansport and bring in a crewman who had murdered a man from a competing boat with a hatchet during a race between the two towns.[153] Citizens of the various towns on the canal were alarmed at the moral void along their waterfronts. When a missionary from the Western Seaman's Friend Society showed up on the Wabash in 1840 at the behest of some of the locals, he soon left, declaring that "there is more outbreaking wickedness here than on any other thoroughfare of equal magnitude in the Union."[154]

Newspapers periodically bemoaned the fights and sinful behavior centered on the taverns at the waterfront, although they apparently

---

151 Bodurtha, *History of Miami County*, 249.
152 Fatout, *Indiana Canals*, 131.
153 Ibid.
154 Ibid.

were not immune from its effects. The May 23, 1850, issue of the *Miami County Sentinel* marked the launching of a canal boat named the *Peruvian* with a brief but flowery article extolling the details of the celebration. The article explained that since the reporter was the most distinguished guest present, he was invited to the "old log shop" (a tavern) where, "overpowered by excitement and corn juice, he became utterly oblivious to things terrestrial, and lost his notes, which is our apology for the meager [sic] account we have given of this imposing spectacle."[155] Not all canal workers behaved poorly, but the wild and wooly behavior along the docks reinforced the troubling notion that the canal was introducing social and environmental changes that people could not control.

Even more disturbing were the illnesses that spread along the canal. They only served to emphasize the weakness of human control over the environment. Sickness stemmed from two sources. One was the transmission of various illnesses up and down the canal by the crews who routinely went east and south to large ports, especially New Orleans. Cholera was highly feared, and the newspapers carried regular updates on where outbreaks occurred as well as advertisements for the latest remedy. In August 1849, *The Miami County Sentinel* stated that there was no cholera in Peru but that it was "bad at Huntington and on the increase in Huntington and Toledo."[156] Another report admonished Peruvians to be "clean about your premises and persons, avoid all green fruits and vegetables …. And observe regularity of habits."[157]

New Orleans was the southern terminus for much of the grain shipped on the canal and faced outbreaks of deadly diseases such as cholera and yellow fever. A series of epidemics in the city, culminating with a yellow fever outbreak in 1853 that killed over ten thousand people, prompted a change in the way people looked at their relationship

---

155 *Miami County Sentinel*, May 23, 1850.
156 Ibid., August 2, 1849.
157 Ibid., July 7, 1849.

with the river "and what they called nature."[158] There were never any outbreaks along the Wabash & Erie Canal that rivaled the deaths in New Orleans, but death from cholera did claim numerous lives along the canal. Fort Wayne suffered outbreaks in 1849, 1852, and 1854. Contemporary newspaper accounts relate the apprehension each year as the disease worked its way up the canal line.[159] These periodic outbreaks were especially unnerving because they showed that the canal introduced changes to the river valley that humans could not control.

Other health problems stemmed from the nature of the canal itself and the carelessness of the people who used it. Many factories and houses stood close to the canal. As the canal grew more urban, it became increasingly polluted. The canal was a dump for trash, garbage, and both human and animal waste. In the summer, disease-carrying mosquitoes proliferated in stagnant canal water. This led to many outbreaks of diarrhea, diphtheria, and other contagions, many with canal-specific names. DeWitt C. Goodrich was born in Miami County, but his family moved to Kansas in 1855 because of the health problems along the Wabash River. He remembered "nearly everybody was initiated into the disagreeable and discouraging intricacies of fever and ague, commonly known the country over as the 'Wabash Shakes.' Few escaped this miasmatic scourge. My father concluded to get away from it ..."[160] Newspapers carried ads for pills and potions guaranteed to cure the various ailments of the local populace. One of the favorites in the Peru papers was Dr. Bragg's Fever and Ague Pills, "HARD TO BEAT!" The pills "swept everything before them ...in the cure of Ague, Billious[sic], and Chill Fevers."[161]

The health problems inherent to the canal were a direct result

---

158   Kelman, *A River and Its City*, 89.
159   *Fort Wayne Sentinel,* January 4, 1845.
160   George W. Martin, ed., *Collections of the Kansas State Historical Society, Vol. XII* (Topeka: State Printing Office, 1912), 388.
161   *Miami County Sentinel,* July 12, 1849.

of the mistaken belief that people could change the landscape while remaining separate from it. Ari Kelman, speaking of the 1853 yellow fever epidemic in New Orleans, explained that even though the people of that city thought they had engineered away many of their problems, the epidemic proved that the nonhuman world could resist "everyday decisions made by people who sought to impose social, economic, and spatial order on their environment."[162] That is exactly what the people along the canal were trying to do. They built the canal to create a new country and economy. On one hand, it was wildly successful, bringing an economic boom to Miami County. On the other hand, it also defied attempts by the populace to confine it within the boundaries set by nineteenth century engineering and became a leaky, weed-choked, unhealthy, corrupting influence on the upper Wabash Valley. Humans had attempted to separate what was man-made from what wasn't and found that it was a difficult thing to do. Many people quit referring to it as the Wabash & Erie Canal and simply called it "The Ditch."[163]

Despite its drawbacks, the canal remained an economic boon to the city of Peru from the 1840s until the railroads caused its decline in the 1850s. The industrial growth of the town traced a narrow path that paralleled the river. Industry spread west from the feeder dam for approximately one and a half miles along Canal Street. The town became more urbanized as the economic infrastructure expanded. An editorial in the July 27, 1848, edition of the *Miami County Sentinel* sang the praises of Peru, calling it "the favored spot of creation," and the author proudly enumerated a long list of businesses to prove the point.[164] The town boasted of dry goods stores, tin shops, drugstores, carpenters, cabinet and chair shops, blacksmiths, a hatter, shoe stores, saddler and wagon maker shops, carding machines, sawmills, gristmills,

162 Kelman, *A River and Its City*, 89.
163 *Miami County Sentinel*, June 17, 1852.
164 *Miami County Sentinel*, July 27, 1848.

"and almost every kind of manufactures in such abundance."[165] There were at least three brick business houses on Broadway and frame houses in every direction "where once stood the neat log cabin." The town population was listed at 1,005, while the county had 7,000 residents, a rapid growth rate for the time. The paper was proud of the numbers and haughtily pointed out that not only could the town provide for the entire county population, they had "sufficient surplus to furnish all the little villages east of us along the canal."[166] In reference to agriculture within Miami County, the article pointed out the large number of grain warehouses on the canal "with capital to purchase, and capacity to store, all the grain we raise" because of the fertility of the soil and dedication of local farmers. The article ended with a reference to the elements of greatness within Peru, claiming that, if necessary, the town could "live perfectly independent of the rest of the world, were we surrounded by a Chinese wall …" if necessary.[167] This was Manifest Destiny at work. Peruvians had taken "a favored spot of creation" and bent it to the economic will of a new landscape.

The editor of the *Sentinel* didn't realize it at the time, but the rise of an agricultural economy in the region would eventually make the people of Peru wish they were indeed "surrounded by a Chinese wall." Peru was in the midst of an economic boom by the 1850s; people poured into Miami County because of the accessibility to cheap land along the canal. The rich, fertile farmland the *Sentinel* bragged about lured settlers to the area. The canal made it easy to get the implements and supplies they needed to clear the land and start farms, as well as market the products grown on those farms. As a result, hundreds of thousands of acres in Miami County and all along the upper Wabash Valley were cleared and converted to crop production. The upper Wabash Valley had originally been covered with timber and wetlands, but by 1860, 1,211,000 acres

165 Ibid.
166 Ibid.
167 Ibid.

in the area had been improved, almost 50 percent of the total acreage. [168] Miami County comprised 384 square miles, or 245,760 acres of that total.[169] When the county was created in 1834, approximately 64,835 acres of it was wetlands with almost 16,500 of those acres permanently covered with water. That translates to 27 percent of the total acreage. Cass County was almost 37 percent wetlands, and other counties along the Wabash had similar percentages.[170]

In its natural state, the land along the upper Wabash Valley worked like a sponge, soaking up rainfall and runoff and allowing it to work its way gradually down to the Wabash River. There was very little erosion, and the slow drainage helped to prevent wide swings in the depth of the river. The Mound builders, the Miami Indians, and other people who lived in the region before 1832 left a very small footprint on the land. Their agricultural methods were on too small a scale to alter the landscape, and when the river flooded, they simply moved to higher ground. The Wabash & Erie Canal altered the environment dramatically. It conveyed thousands of land-hungry immigrants into the area who cleared the land and built ditches to drain it.

As early as 1845, George Winter, the Hoosier artist who documented Miami Indian life, moved to Logansport. He noted "the effects of the partial clearing of the country." [171] He wrote in his journal that the rapid clearing of land "has had a striking effect on the affluents [sic] of the Wabash" and that "the beautiful islands are beginning to wash away under the influence of the greater volume of water that fills the banks and the increased rapidity of the current of the river."[172] The amount

---

168 Carter, "Rural Indiana,"109.

169 Brant, *History of Miami County*, 272.

170 Alton A. Lindsey, "Vegetation of the Drainage-Aeration Classes of Northern Indiana Soils in 1830," *Ecology* 42.2 (1961), 432.

171 Gammon, *Wabash River Ecosystem*, 13.

172 Ibid.

of silts and clays in the bottom also increased greatly.[173] The Wabash River felt the impact, becoming more turbid and erratic in discharge. The agricultural boom caused by the canal changed the landscape of the upper Wabash Valley more in fifty years than it had in the prior fifty thousand. The Wa-Ba-Shiki would never be clear again.

The growth of Miami County occurred at a furious pace. The value of taxable property in the county grew from $401,354 in 1841 to $4,265,763 in 1860, a tenfold increase.[174] Men built and improved roads on a regular basis, allowing rural areas better access to Peru, but farmers wanted one improvement above all others: drainage for their cropland. The building of ditches and installation of tiles proceeded at a furious pace, opening vast tracts of land to cultivation. The same thing happened in other counties, and agricultural output in the region skyrocketed. In 1844, the Wabash & Erie Canal shipped 5,000 bushels of corn to the port in Toledo. By 1846, the number increased to 500,000, and in 1851, 2,775,149 bushels of corn traveled up the canal to Toledo.[175] The change was dramatic, but what was seen by most people as an improvement was also an attempt to impose human economic and spatial order on the environment.

The consequences of environmental change to the Wabash River affected every city along the canal, but none more than Peru. In their efforts to develop Miami County, residents destabilized the natural ability of the land to control the flow of water into the Wabash and Mississinewa Rivers. Will Hundley was a young man when his family moved to Miami County in 1875 to teach farming to what was left of the Miami Indians in the area. They lived in a place the locals called Squawtown, in the rich bottomland where the Mississinewa and Wabash Rivers met. The area contained large stands of timber, but the

---

173   Arthur C. Benke, Colbert E. Cushing, *Rivers of North America: The Natural History* (Burlington, MA: Academic Press, 2005), 388.

174   Brant, *History of Miami County*, 282.

175   Gammon, *Wabash River Ecosystem*, 16.

forests were disappearing rapidly as teams of men worked daily cutting cordwood to feed the boilers of the Peru Brewery and other businesses. Even as a young boy, Hundley lamented the loss of the trees and recalled in later years the "grief at seeing an axe sink into their bodies" as dozens of axmen denuded the countryside cutting firewood for Peru.[176]

He was watching a great environmental change in the local landscape. One long-term consequence of nineteenth-century deforestation of the area was noted when a 1911 soil survey showed a complete absence of water storage capacity due to the lack of wooded land and drainage efforts. "The land has been systematically drained, and the forests removed ... Before the land was artificially drained there was considerable natural storage ... the discharge of the Mississinewa River is very irregular."[177] In an effort to manage the flow of water along the upper Wabash Valley, humans created even more destabilization of the rivers they sought to control.

John Stephens said in 1896 that drainage was one of the indexes by which to "gauge the civilization of a country."[178] Both he and Arthur Bodurtha devote chapters of their respective Miami County histories to the subject of drainage, reflecting the importance of the subject to local history but missing the environmental consequences of unbridled expansion. Bodurtha looked back in 1914 and wrote of the recollections of some of the old settlers. They could remember when spring brought heavy rains and melting snow, turning the countryside into a morass. Much of the county consisted of wetlands that in their natural state "were the source of much of the fever and ague with which the early settlers had to contend." Those same settlers were determined to rid themselves of those wetlands. Farmers dug hundreds of miles of ditches

---

176 Will M. Hundley, *Squawtown: My Boyhood Among the Last Miami Indians* (Caldwell, ID: Caxton Printers, 1939), 95.

177 Indiana Department of Geology and Natural Resources, *Indiana Geological Survey. 36th Annual Report of Department of Geology and Natural Resources* (Indianapolis: State of Indiana, 1911), 514.

178 Stephens, *History of Miami County*, 102.

in order to make the land usable. By 1869, a more efficient way of draining land emerged with the introduction of a clay tile system of drainage, and most of Miami County's wetlands quickly disappeared, destroying the buffer needed to prevent spring runoff from reaching the rivers all at once. In the eyes of the local historian, "Drainage has not only improved the land for agricultural purposes … it has also improved the health of the county's inhabitants."[179] The fact that this was still the prevailing view in 1914, when Bodurtha wrote, reinforces the view that no one truly understood the real cost of tinkering with the landscape around Peru.

The rapid draining of hundreds of thousands of acres of land had an immediate impact on the Wabash River. The erosion George Winter observed in the spring of 1845 was soon evident everywhere and only increased with time. The river got muddier as banks caved in, and floods became more frequent. Unlike the Miami Indians, the residents of Peru, Wabash, Logansport, and other towns along the river couldn't just pack up and move to high ground when the river flooded. Most of the industry and commerce in these towns was concentrated close to the canal, which put much of the local economy at the mercy of the Wabash River. Peru was in an exceptionally vulnerable spot because of its proximity to the confluence of the Wabash and Mississinewa Rivers. This location aggravated the chances for severe damage from flooding. The industrial center for the town grew up by the feeder dam for the canal, an extremely vulnerable position less than a mile downriver from where the two rivers met. But, the site was large and well suited for industry, with easy access to water power.

If not for the dam, Miamisport would probably have been the county seat, and Peru would not have been built. Industry would have been located another two miles downstream from the mouth of the Mississinewa, but in 1834 no one worried about the potential for major

---

179 Bodurtha, *History of Miami County*, 264.

flood damage because there was no known pattern to suggest it was a problem. Unfortunately for the people who lived along the upper Wabash Valley, the behavior of the river became more unpredictable with each tree that was felled and every ditch that was dug. Erratic water levels triggered a sequence of events that conflicted with the assumptions that citizens had made about human control of the landscape around Peru.

Technology produced the canal, but it couldn't guarantee the cooperation of nature. Engineering fixed broken banks, but groundhogs burrowed right back through them. Workers built dams to create reservoirs for the canal, but they couldn't make it rain, nor stop it once it started. Chief Cha-pine was prescient when he snorted in disgust at the ditch Jesse Williams wanted to run through his parlor. The idea that man could tame the power of the Wabash River with a canal was self-defeating. The Wabash & Erie Canal was not separate from the landscape of the upper Wabash Valley; it simply became part of it. Each whiskey-swilling, feverish canal boat crewman proved it. What was human along the Wabash and what was natural was difficult to separate. The settlers along the river altered their environment, but nature had the capacity, in turn, to change what humans did, shifting the definition of landscape. Failure to appreciate the capacity of nature to adapt to a changing landscape blinded the people of Peru to the consequences of building their town where they did. It was only when nature pushed back and almost destroyed the town during the 1913 flood that people began to perceive the true relationship with the Wabash River.

CHAPTER 3
Railroads, Floods, and Disaster

T HE 1913 FLOOD DISASTER WAS THE CULMINATION OF DECADES OF misperception about the relationship between Peru and the Wabash River. From the very beginning, economic considerations dictated the site of the town without regard for the potential of the river to destroy it. The Wabash & Erie Canal in general and Feeder Dam Number Three in particular promised great economic expansion for both Peru and the surrounding area. As a result, there was a dramatic increase in population, the conversion of thousands of acres of natural wetlands into farmland by the introduction of drainage tiles and irrigation ditches, and the spread of industry along the Wabash River. The residents of the area saw these changes as signs of progress although there was evidence that economic changes were accompanied by less desirable social and environmental consequences.

Human attempts to control the landscape through technology were ineffective. Nature continually interfered with the canal, causing expensive delays and repairs to the system. When the railroad, a technologically superior transportation method, took over, it brought its own set of problems to the landscape. Human tinkering with the natural drainage of the area contributed to changes along the Wabash River and increased the damage caused by periodic flooding.

Eventually, the 1913 flood devastated Peru, defining both a physical and economic high-water mark that was never surpassed, as well as exposing the misconception that the residents of the town controlled the landscape surrounding them. William Hood built his town on the premise that man could overcome nature and harness it for economic gain, using "the natural and artificial resources which Peru has under control."[180]

At first, the canal was the principal manifestation of human control of local resources, but technological advances during the nineteenth century soon made it obsolete. The landscape evolved as humans sought more control over the transportation system that drove the economic engine of the area. A more reliable form of transportation, the railroad, replaced the canal. Men cleared and drained land, and the city of Peru grew, but environmental changes that accompanied the process were neglected for the most part until the Wabash River became increasingly erratic, teaching the lesson that new technology does not always equal more environmental control.

Railroads emerged as the technologically superior form of transportation in the 1850s, causing the canal to begin losing money. The original purpose of the canal as an economic engine for the Wabash Valley was tempered by the reality that it had many drawbacks as a mode of transportation when compared to the railroad. The economic success of the canal was dependent on water. While the canal was physically separate from the river, it was susceptible to seasonal as well as less predictable changes of the Wabash. Even before the canal system was completed, the fledgling railroad industry loomed as a potent, more reliable method of transportation in the region, causing canal fever to gradually fade away in favor of the railroads.

---

180   Clarence E. Weaver, *A Description of the City of Peru, Miami County, Indiana* (Peru, IN: The Indiana Advancement Company, 1897), 5.

The advantages of railroads over canals were numerous. Railroads operated twelve months out of the year, provided direct transportation to cities not connected by canals, and were more reliable than the leaky, high-maintenance canal beds. Moreover, canal boats were forced to creep along at speeds under five miles per hour to prevent a bow wave and subsequent erosion of the banks. Most canal cargo also had to be transferred from boat to boat before arriving at its destination, while rail cargo rarely needed transshipment. Trains were much faster and offered the added benefit of greater cargo capacity, meaning cheaper rates and faster service.

These facts were not lost on the town fathers in Peru. The canal brought the first wave of farmers and industry to the area and defined the geography of the town, but it was the railroads that ultimately capitalized on the strong agricultural trade established with eastern markets. Even as the Wabash & Erie Canal fueled the growth of Miami County during the 1840s, many voices embraced the idea of making Peru a major rail terminal. By 1849, Peru newspapers carried the public debate on whether the county should vote for a $20,000 subscription to start a rail line from Indianapolis to Peru. Voters approved, but the money soon ran out. It took almost five more years for investors to raise enough capital for completion of the line. It was a process occurring across the state. Between 1850 and 1860, investors spent over $34,000,000, and railroad mileage in Indiana expanded from 228 miles to 2,163 miles.[181]

The construction of the rail lines in and around Peru altered the urban landscape in key ways, expanding the industrial base within the town as well as altering the natural floodplain for both the Mississinewa and Wabash Rivers. The Peru & Indianapolis Railroad finally reached Peru in the spring of 1854, opening a new era in transportation, dooming the canal to a slow death, and expanding the economic base of Peru

---

181   Stephen S. Visher, *Economic Geography of Indiana* (New York: D. Appleton, 1923), 102.

with hundreds of railroad-related jobs.[182] The Indianapolis-Peru line was quickly followed by another railroad company, the Wabash, St. Louis, & Pacific Railway, formed with the intention of building a line down the length of the Wabash Valley from Toledo to St. Louis. When asked to speak about the advisability of building this line, Daniel Pratt, a wealthy Logansport businessman, signed a sizable check to the new rail company, commenting "There is my speech."[183] Other people agreed, and the line was soon under way, making Peru a major rail hub in the process. Over the ensuing years, at least five railroads built lines through Peru, but the Indianapolis and Wabash are the two lines that had the greatest economic and environmental impact on Miami County.

The immediate consequence of the transition to rail transportation was the diversification of industry within Peru. By the time the Wabash & Erie Canal was abandoned in 1875, Peru's main industrial area was well established along the Wabash River. The area along the old feeder dam contained a woolen mill, a distillery, and a massive seven-acre complex built for the Howe Sewing Machine Company. Various peripheral businesses were also located there. It remained the most concentrated industrial area in the city. Stretching along the river farther to the west were a number of large planing, saw, bagging, and woolen mills, as well as breweries, a foundry, and various smaller factories manufacturing everything from cabinets to wheels.

Some of the businesses depended on water power, but not all. An abundance of locally cut wood made steam power a viable alternative, and many industries went that route. Others took advantage of the introduction of natural gas in 1874. By 1879, a new bridge over the Wabash River on Broadway opened up South Peru to industry, and various small manufacturers soon moved there as well.[184]

---

182 Bodurtha, *History of Miami County*, 254–55.
183 Ibid., 256.
184 Marilyn Coppernoll, *Miami County, Indiana: A Pictorial History* (Virginia Beach, VA: Donning, 1995), 25.

The Indianapolis-Peru railroad supported the older industries because the line was built partially on the old canal bed, continuing to provide convenient access for the loading and unloading of cargo. It also provided an opportunity for new industrial areas to flourish as spur lines reached out to new factories. The Wabash line cut across the north side of Peru, and industry soon gravitated to it. The area was attractive in part because it was away from the river. Only once in the past, in 1847, had floodwaters been deep enough to reach the ridge north of town, and in the 1850s the city dug a large ditch around the north side of town for the express purpose of rerouting floodwater away from the area in order to make the location safe for expansion. Warehouses, a new depot, and repair facilities for the railroad provided a nexus for the new industrial district.

By 1875 the growth of the railroads made Peru's economy much less reliant on water power, and, as a result, the nature of the relationship between the town and the river changed. The Wabash & Erie Canal, awash in red ink, was finally abandoned by the state in the face of competition from the railroads. The area along Canal Street, once looked upon with pride by Peruvians as the economic heart of the town, was worn around the edges. The feeder dam washed out late that year and was never repaired.[185] Long stretches of the canal remained, but lack of maintenance turned them into stagnant pools of water, which brought nothing but complaints from the townsfolk.[186]

The separation of the river and the town increased when the railroad took over the old canal bed, ending the economic dependency on water and making many of the warehouses and businesses along Canal Street obsolete. Heavy industry still dominated the area, but many new businesses moved into other parts of town, leaving the once-thriving waterfront to deteriorate. The Wabash River overflowed periodically,

---

185 Thomas E. Castaldi, *Wabash & Erie Canal Notebook III: Wabash and Miami Counties* (Fort Wayne, IN: Parrot Printing, 2004), 151.

186 Stephens, *History of Miami County*, 128.

leaving a foot or so of water along Canal Street, making a mess and costing businesses money. Canal Street lost its luster, and the Wabash River became increasingly irrelevant to town planning as it diminished in economic importance. As a result, the people ignored the natural role the river played in the urban, industrial, and agricultural landscape they created. As people implemented these changes along the river valley, unintended environmental changes accompanied the process.

Train coming into Peru on the raised railbed east of town
(Photo courtesy of the Miami County, Indiana, Historical Society)

When engineers built the first rail lines in the 1850s and 1860s, they gave little consideration to what might happen if the Wabash flooded because they didn't fully understand the pronounced effect of agricultural drainage into the river. Floods in Peru were generally mild and confined to the waterfront. As a result, the potential environmental impact of railbed design on the land was ignored. Mid-nineteenth century construction techniques were simple and effective. Engineers saw the laying of rail lines as an exercise in rising above topographical problems presented by the natural landscape, so they did just that, they rose above. The railbed was almost always raised above ground level in what was known as the Whittemore form, a standard construction technique of the time that allowed for a stable and easily drained foundation.[187] The end result was a sloped mound about thirty feet wide at the bottom and roughly ten to twelve feet wide at the top. On level terrain, the bed would be five to eight feet high. In other words, the roadbed design also doubled as a sturdy dike, capable of diverting massive amounts of water if constructed across a floodplain like that at the confluence of the Wabash and Mississinewa Rivers.

Engineers did not see this as a major problem at the time. William Raymond's 1914 bible for railroad construction, *The Elements of Railroad Engineering*, makes no mention of environmental consequences of railroad construction. There was no consideration of potential flooding, only normal drainage. The only nod to the potential power of water in the manual was the recommendation that ditches at least one foot deep be preserved when digging dirt for the rail embankment from what was known as a borrow pit. In that way, the raised railbed would have "thorough drainage and freedom from snow drifts" as well as provide a way for natural runoff, although normally (according to engineers of the time), "the matter will usually take care of itself."[188] This was the basic construction method used when the first rail lines reached out toward Peru.

The engineers were not careless when they failed to factor in the hydraulic power of the Wabash River on a landscape being dissected by both railroads and modern drainage systems; they just had an incomplete understanding of the relationship between rivers and the man-made landscape in general. What seemed simple was not.[189] The inhabitants

187 William Galt Raymond, *The Elements of Railroad Engineering* (New York: John Wiley & Sons, 1914), 53–56.
188 Ibid., 55–56.
189 Richard White, *The Organic Machine: The Remaking of the Columbia River* (New York: Hill and Wang, 1995), 30.

of Miami County blissfully crisscrossed the countryside with roads, rails, ditches, drains, and tiles, unaware that their relationship with the natural world was not simply one of control, but rather a complicated interaction that affected the environment in unforeseen ways.

Peru was firmly established as a rail and business center by 1875. Thanks to the legacy of the canal, economic output was strong, with Wabash, Miami, and Cass Counties consistently ranked in the top tier of wage distribution for the state.[190] The population grew slowly but consistently, and passed 4,000 at about this time.[191] The boundaries of the town expanded along the river to accommodate growth, and by 1875 Peru reached the basic form that it retains to the present day. In just over forty years, settlers transformed untrammeled wetlands and forests into an orderly, industrious town hugging the banks of the Wabash.

Peru in the mid-nineteenth century
(Photo courtesy of the Miami County, Indiana, Historical Society)

190 George W. Starr, *Industrial Development of Indiana* (Bloomington: Indiana University School of Business Administration, 1937), 53–55.
191 Brant and Fuller, *History of Miami County*, 371.

An 1897 description of the community shows that the citizens of Peru were proud of the town and saw their handiwork as the result of the ability of man to control nature: "From the day of its foundation, Peru has been prosperous, and has grown entirely through force of circumstances and has attained its prominence through *natural causes alone*."[192] "Force of circumstances" was just another way of saying Manifest Destiny on a local scale. Peruvians had succeeded because of their natural ability to harness and exploit the resources around them, especially the river. The same volume also claims "that the city has reached its present position upon a foundation secure beyond per-adventure is but a convincing proof of the certainty with which nature secures her ends."[193] Again, it was a recognition of nature, but one that split the definition of the word in two. To the pioneers who had seen the changes their axes and saws made to the land, Peru represented the transformation of traditional nature into a superior, final form they identified as human civilization. The assumption was that the wilderness was conquered by the pioneers and that nature now existed to serve the needs of man.

It was a costly misperception to believe that human society could separate Peru from the Wabash River. Many of the technological advances that Peruvians looked proudly to as proof that nature was tamed were, in reality, evidence that the dividing line between the Wabash River and the town was tenuous at best. Starting with the Wabash & Erie Canal and extending to the new railroads that replaced it, the citizens of the upper Wabash Valley utilized the new transportation system to fuel tremendous growth in the agricultural output of the region. As a result of this growth, the main function of the Wabash River changed from that of transportation to one of drainage for newly cleared farmland. The installation of ditches and drains along the Upper Wabash River Valley reveals that the agricultural experts and hydrological engineers

---

192 Weaver, *Description of the City*, 3. Italics added.
193 Ibid.

of the time continued to see the local environment as a resource they could manipulate and control at will.

The statewide movement to modernize transportation and drain the land grew in scope as the years passed. In 1875, the Indiana state legislature passed the first of a number of laws outlining the procedures for installing drainage ditches and tiles. Farmers had been draining cropland for decades, but this was the first mechanism instituted by the state to organize and control the effort. By 1893, the system evolved into a coordinated arrangement to build and maintain the thousands of miles of ditches and tiles in Indiana, but little effort was expended by state engineers in determining the environmental impact of the work. By 1890, more than 1.5 million acres of Indiana swampland was drained.[194] By 1895, Indiana had over thirty thousand miles of tile and ditches.[195] In 1896, Miami County alone had 204 miles of main-line drainage ditches. This number did not include the satellite branches connected to the major ones.[196] Each town along the river also built sewer systems to divert rainwater into the river. Almost two-thirds of the state (32,600 square miles) drained into the Wabash River, and as the years passed, the river level tended to be more erratic than in the past.[197] Runoff that used to take months to flow down to the Wabash now reached the river in a matter of days.

Coupled with erosion caused by the rapid deforestation of the watershed, the increased amount of runoff put mounting pressure on the Wabash. The US Geological Survey in 1896 recognized that changes were occurring to the river: "The effect of settlement has been to afford better surface drainage by opening ditches and removing obstructions, and thus to lessen the amount of saturation. Cultivation of fields, leading

---

194 Charles Kettleborough, *Drainage and Reclamation of Swamp and Overflowed Lands: Indiana Bureau of Legislative Information, Bulletin No. 2* (Indianapolis: State of Indiana, 1914), 13.

195 Ibid., 46.

196 Bodurtha, *History of Miami County*, 265–66.

197 Kettleborough, *Drainage and Reclamation*, 46.

as it usually does to a more rapid escape of water over the surface, also tends to lessen the degree of saturation."[198] The USGS survey drew no specific conclusions about the meaning of the findings, and the significance of the impact on the Wabash River was not addressed in the report, but the rapid escape of surface water meant higher average river levels during the spring runoff, leaving lower levels in the summer. The average summer flow of the river fell from an estimated 6,740 cfs (cubic feet per second) in 1833 to only 3,750 cfs by 1881.[199] The average spring flow is not mentioned in the survey, but according to National Weather Service records, there were floods in Peru approximately fourteen times between 1847 and 1913. These were floods exceeding twenty feet, the flood stage for the Wabash River at Peru.[200]

There is no better way to illustrate the cumulative effect of the environmental changes that took place in the vicinity of Peru than by looking at the changes in the Wabash River beginning in the second half of the nineteenth century. The seasonal swings in water levels became stronger, resulting in increasingly powerful flooding along the Wabash. The rising threat of flooding also caused a shift in the way people saw the river. The residents of the area originally ignored the river as anything other than a power source for the local economy, but the change in the behavior of the Wabash caused a shift in perception. The river came to represent a danger to the economy of the region, especially the vulnerable industrial district in Peru.

By cross-referencing the NOAA flood dates with the Peru newspapers, it is possible to assess the change in attitude of townspeople toward the place of the river within the landscape as the flooding of the Wabash River increased in severity, evolving from a seasonal nuisance to an

---

198   Frank Leverett, *Water Resources of Indiana and Ohio, U.S. Geological Survey,* vol. IV (Washington, DC: Government Printing Office, 1897), 477.
199   US Government Printing Office, *Annual Report of the Chief of Engineers U.S. Army,* vol. III (1881), 407.
200   National Weather Service, "Advanced Hydrologic Prediction Service," ed. NOAA, 2009.

economic nightmare. Over the latter half of the nineteenth century, the river became increasingly more volatile, but initially the people of Peru considered the temperamental nature of the Wabash as a normal part of life. There was no serious attempt made by the original inhabitants of Peru to guard against the seasonal vagaries of the river because the flooding was usually minor and was accepted by locals as an occasional intrusion by nature, not a loss of control over the environment. The local papers carried neither an outcry for flood control nor complaints about the river. Contemporary newspapers don't even mention many of the minor floods of the mid-nineteenth century, lending credence to the idea that floods were seen by Peruvians as a minor inconvenience not worth mentioning. They brought a few inches of water to Canal Street and associated areas, and usually retreated in a few hours. If the newspaper accounts mention them at all, it is in a perfunctory manner that offered little information about damage. These floods resulted in roughly ten to fourteen inches of water overflowing the banks of the Wabash with minor damage to businesses and varying levels of crop damage, depending on the time of year. It was a nuisance but not a serious challenge to human control of the landscape.

On at least six different occasions, however, major floods challenged the perception that humans were in control.[201] Local newspaper accounts all agree that the first major flood to hit Peru was in January 1847. It was caused by an ice dam on the river, but there are few contemporary descriptions of the event. Most accounts were related by the town's old-timers during later floods. The next major flood of note to hit Peru after 1847 was in August 1875.

---

201 Those floods occurred in 1847, 1875, 1883, 1904, 1907, and 1913. All of them, with the exception of the 1913 flood, varied in height from two to three feet over flood stage. The 1913 flood was a major disaster, reaching a flood stage of almost nine feet.

One of the earliest flood photos of Peru, believed to be of the 1875 flood
(Photo courtesy of the Miami County, Indiana, Historical Society)

Although contemporary accounts fail to mention it, this one was unusual because most of the floods hit during what was known as the annual "freshet," an old term for the spring thaw and the heavy rains that accompanied it. The 1875 flood, caused by a few days of torrential downpours, demonstrated the increasing volatility of the Wabash River. It was the first large summer flood to hit the town. By 1875, Peru and the surrounding rural area had grown to the point where a flood could do some major damage.

The August flood did just that. The newspaper defined it in biblical terms, calling it a "Deluge" and claiming: "Shades of Father Noah Invoked, Demand for Gopher Wood or any Ark Timber."[202] While the headlines were tongue-in-cheek, the byline was serious, mentioning "Fearful Losses in the Wabash Valley."[203] At Peru, the Mississinewa River exploded over the north bank of the Wabash at their confluence and spread over the lowlands on the north side of the river, even submerging

202 *Miami County Sentinel,* August 6, 1875.
203 Ibid.

portions of the railroad tracks running between Peru and Wabash. The newspaper claimed the high-water mark to be less than two feet from the 1847 flood, but considered the 1875 flood to be worse: "Then [1847] the river was full of ice, the channel was narrow and the passage of the water obstructed much more than during the recent freshet."[204] The consensus was that the 1875 flood involved a much larger volume of water despite the fact that the 1847 flood was higher. No article mentioned the impact of man-made changes to the watershed, or offered any explanation for the unusual timing of the event.

In what would become a trend over the ensuing years, the 1875 newspaper accounts listed various businesses and the damage they incurred. The Howe Manufacturing plant at the old feeder dam was flooded with three feet of water, and much of their lumber was swept away. Other factories had lumber or other inventory washed away. The entire downtown business district received water damage of some kind. South Peru, being several feet lower than the ground north of the river, suffered even worse flooding.[205] Losses in the rural areas around Peru were also high. Corn crops were drowned and most of the season's wheat crop was still in the field, drying in shocks. It was all destroyed.[206] The floodwaters devastated most of the Wabash Valley, wiping it clean. When the flood was over, men found an old canal boat wedged against the railroad bridge in west Peru. No one knew where it came from, but it had undoubtedly been abandoned somewhere along the old canal bed east of Peru and swept away when the flood washed away the banks of the canal in many places. The flood also destroyed most of the old feeder dam, reclaiming what man had built, erasing much of the imaginary line between man and nature, and putting an exclamation point on the finale of the Wabash & Erie Canal in Peru.[207]

---

204 Ibid.
205 Ibid.
206 Ibid., August 20, 1875.
207 *The Peru Sentinel*, August 12, 1875.

No one put a dollar amount on the losses caused by the 1875 flood, but it was significant because of the growing number of business interests along the river. Many of the industries along the Wabash saw their raw materials and inventory float away, destroying large amounts of uninsured capital. The Howe Sewing Machine Company, employing five hundred people, went bankrupt soon after the flood and was sold by investors to the Indiana Manufacturing Company.[208] Other businesses, unable to absorb their losses, also closed. Crop losses in the lowlands were virtually 100 percent, causing some farms to fail.[209]

The economic impact on Peru was heavy, yet city leaders didn't address the problem. No one perished in the flood, and there was no organized relief system to aid victims after it ended. Other than advice on how to disinfect foul cellars and a reprimand to flood gawkers that "the visitors at the dam last Sunday were more numerous than the visitors at the churches," the newspapers provided no more information about the flood after August 20.[210] Peru soon returned to normal. This flood does not even receive a mention in Arthur Bodurtha's comprehensive history of Peru, published only thirty-nine years after the event.

How could such a significant event be brushed aside so easily? In the case of Peru, the economic die had been cast with the building of the canal. Capital had flowed to the river to take advantage of cheap waterpower from the feeder dam and the transportation network of the canal. The waterfront controlled the destiny of the town, and, in turn, wealthy commercial interests controlled the waterfront from the instant Peru was imagined into existence by William Hood's engineer. Since the town could not be "imagined" into a safer location, the only thing to do was push forward. There was no alternative; too much was at stake to abandon the waterfront because of the river. The river and the populace of Peru traditionally had little contact anyway. The people

---

208 *The Peru Republican*, August 20, 1875.
209 Ibid.
210 Ibid.

of Peru saw flooding as an act of nature that sometimes crossed the dividing line between what was natural and what they had built. As such, they saw it as a temporary nuisance that accompanied their use of nature and not as a permanent threat, so they ignored it. In 1875, that was still an option.

The citizens of the town could ignore the river, but the river refused to ignore them. The more Peru's economy grew, the more problematic the floods became. City fathers wanted to promote Peru as the best location in the region for new commercial interests, but the threat of flooding erased the perceived line between the town and the river and made Peru a very poor choice for investment. Unlike the minor floods of the past, the severity of the 1875 flood created a situation where Peru had nothing to gain and everything to lose if the perception of the river shifted to give it a more prominent role in the landscape. The townspeople could rationalize away the role of humans in the disaster by calling it an act of God. After all, people were helpless "when compared to the terrible power of the nonhuman world, whether 'God' or 'Nature.'"[211] By comparing the 1875 flood to a biblical deluge and inferring that the citizens of Peru needed an ark, the newspapers drew attention away from the fact that the flood damage had more to do with the location of local industry and the impact of farming than it did the will of God.

It was not until the flood of 1883 that townsfolk began to recognize the predicament they were in. The 1883 event was the third major flood to hit Peru. It was also the worst to that point, hitting Peru during the first week of February after three days of heavy sleet and rain accompanied by a massive ice storm. The flood crested about three feet above flood stage and caused damage comparable to the 1875 flood. The *Peru Republican* reported that the rapid rise of the river was due to the fact that a thick coating of ice prevented any water from soaking into

211   Kelman, *A River and Its City*, 112.

the ground.[212] Ice dams on the Wabash further complicated matters. The flood started on Friday, February 2, and crested on Sunday, the Fourth. The paper reported that "never before was such an expanse of country here covered by the Wabash."[213] The Mississinewa again pushed north over the railroad embankment and filled the prairie around Peru with over two feet of water. The reporting of this flood also marks the first time newspapers made mention of the need to rescue people with boats as well as rumors (later proven false) that a family east of town had drowned. It is also the first time that a local relief committee was organized to administer aid to flood victims.[214]

This meant that the local population was beginning to see the floods in a new light. They no longer looked upon floods as a mere nuisance; flooding now affected the personal and working lives of thousands of people. A reporter for the paper visited the Indiana Manufacturing plant and found that the water level had reached three and one-half feet high on the first floor. Workers at the plant had scrambled to secure lumber and equipment, preventing massive damage, although the company still suffered over $5,000 in losses. This time around, the paper carried many personal interest stories about the flood and far less information on what it did to the economy of the town. The headline was "Frost and Flood: Destructive Deluge on the Wabash and the Ohio and the Mississippi Valleys," another allusion to a biblical-style flood.[215] Once again, this reinforced the belief that the flood was an act of God, not a result of human development along the river valley.

The paper also covered in detail the light-hearted discussion among old-timers on whether or not the 1847 or 1883 flood was the worst. Underlying the seemingly frivolous story was the serious question of whether the floods were getting worse. Newspaper accounts during

---

212 *Peru Republican,* February 9, 1883.
213 Ibid.
214 Bodurtha, *History of Miami County,* 400.
215 *Peru Republican,* February 9, 1883.

the flood of 1883 also offer the most information about the 1847 flood because the two were similar in nature, and there were still some of the original settlers from the 1840s alive to compare the two. Both were major floods that caused considerable damage, but many of the old-timers could not agree on which one was the worst. The February 9, 1883, issue of the *Peru Republican* discussed the pros and cons of both arguments. Apparently in 1847 a mark was notched into the trunk of an elm tree between Canal Street and the Wabash River delineating the high-water mark for that flood. During the height of the 1883 flood, "some adventurous young men took a lantern and searched for the old mark on the elm tree and report that it was covered with water."[216] However, many of the riverfront factories and businesses marked the heights and dates of the various floods on their walls, and the 1847 faction pointed to the fact that many of those marks showed the 1883 flood did not measure up, so to speak. The two factions had to agree to disagree, but the general consensus was that the 1883 flood was worse.[217] There were no suggestions in any newspaper on what to do about it.

This newspaper account provides insight into the attitude of Peruvians in 1883. Rather than focusing on the mounting problems caused by flooding, there was an almost perverse pride taken by townspeople in the level of destruction. Townspeople treated the river like a naughty child whose antics could be measured by a mark on a wall or a notch on a tree. Bragging rights took precedence over flood control. Contemporary visions of the landscape simply did not allow the people along the river to recognize that human intrusion into the environment was exacerbating the problem. What Peruvians failed to recognize was that no matter how much they tried to bury nature within the urban landscape of the town, they could only ignore their relationship with the nonhuman world at their own peril. People surely noticed that the marks on the walls were climbing higher and occurring more often than

---

216 *Peru Republican*, February 4, 1883.
217 Ibid.

in the "good old days" of 1847. Whether knowingly or not, by turning the discussion into a contest over which flood was the highest, the article deflected attention from the fact that the floods were affecting the economy and quality of life in Peru. Townspeople ignored the growing flood problem even as they marked its advance on their walls.

Over the next few weeks, articles also appeared in the newspapers that downplayed the severity of the flood. The economic base of the town had grown considerably since 1875, and it was difficult to ignore the significance of the damage, but the local papers tried. On February 16, the paper denied outside reports of damage, claiming that no one in the county lacked fuel or food and that total flood losses for the county would not exceed $20,000.[218] Considering the fact that Indiana Manufacturing alone reported $5,000 in damages, the paper seemed to be shortchanging the scope of the damage. The articles also stressed the speed with which the town returned to normal.

The 1883 flood was undoubtedly the costliest yet to Peru, and despite attempts to minimize the damage, follow-up articles in the *Peru Republican* reveal a dawning awareness by some people that the Wabash was a growing threat to the community. In March 1883, a huge ice dam formed across the river below Peru. It caused continued flooding of bottomlands as water poured around either side of the river. The county council financed several attempts to blow up the dam, but the dynamite had no effect. "The work was reluctantly abandoned, but council in its power did everything to satisfy the demand of the people …"[219] This is an admission in print that some in the community were giving voice to their concerns over the river.

Demand for change was not the dominant position of the time, however; denial was still the prevalent attitude. A February newspaper article discounted the sensationalistic reports made in neighboring towns about the damage caused to Peru by the 1883 flood. "One report was

218   Ibid., February 16, 1883.
219   Ibid., March 2, 1883.

circulated that the Dow works [north of Peru] were submerged and … that the water was up to the courthouse. *It will be a wet day in Peru when either of these things takes place.*"[220] This defiant quote reinforced the notion that people controlled the economic and environmental agenda in Peru, and for a number of years the newspaper was right. No one realized that the prediction would be fulfilled in 1913.

After 1883, Peru received a temporary respite from severe flooding. Although sporadic minor floods were common, twenty-one years passed before the next big event occurred. Memories of 1883 faded, and, once again, the idea of a major flood became easy to ignore. Two of Peru's richest men, Milton Shirk and Aaron Dukes, bought the entire stretch of the Wabash & Erie Canal between Huntington and Lafayette when it was sold for pennies on the dollar by the state during the bankruptcy sale for the defunct waterway. They planned on selling the narrow strip of land to industry and railroads, so acknowledging the vulnerability of their investment to the power of the river would impede sales. They did their best to downplay potential problems, even taking over the most consistently flood-ravaged industrial site in Peru, the Indiana Manufacturing complex, down by the old feeder dam, to ensure it remained in business.

By 1900, potential environmental problems abounded around Peru. The Wabash Railroad ran across the prairie north of the confluence of the Wabash and Mississinewa Rivers while the Lake Erie & Western Railroad (later the Chesapeake & Ohio) ran from Indianapolis north to Peru. Both of these lines employed the elevated rail bed of the Whittemore form, and each was raised after the 1883 flood showed they were inadequate. This meant that the flood plain on both the north and south sides of the confluence of the Wabash and Mississinewa Rivers was blocked by a five-feet-eight-high railbed that doubled as a dam.

---

220   Ibid., February 23, 1883. Italics added.

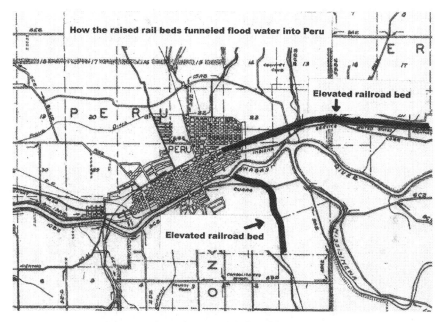

Map showing how the raised railroad beds leading into
Peru funneled floodwater directly into the town
(Map courtesy of the author)

The main consequence of this action was the creation of a large impoundment area between the two railroads. If the rivers flooded, instead of immediately flowing out to the north and south foothills of the Wabash Valley, the water would be stopped by the elevated rails and funneled directly toward the city of Peru. If the flow from the Mississinewa River was powerful enough, it would, in time, overwhelm the Wabash Railroad tracks and flow north and west, hitting the town from that direction also. By 1900, Peru was at the mouth of a double-barreled shotgun in the form of the two rivers. All they needed to trigger a disaster was the right conditions.

The people of Peru did not fully comprehend the threat from the continued changes to the environment. Farmers rapidly put new land under the plow, and more products found their way to market at Peru. The city embraced the railroads with the same fervor originally directed at the Wabash & Erie Canal. Railroads not only provided hundreds of jobs for Peruvians, they maintained the economic growth of the town by providing cheap transportation for the agricultural and manufactured goods produced in and around the rapidly industrializing town. By 1904, the population of Peru had grown to over 10,500.[221] The small village was on the verge of becoming a major industrial center.

Broadway and Canal Street intersection in the early 1900's
(Photo courtesy of the Miami County, Indiana, Historical Society)

If the original marriage between Peru and the canal had been one of man and nature, the introduction of modern industry seemed to delineate a permanent separation of the two. Man no longer needed nature. "The machine ... was their surrogate in what seemed a simple opposition of the mechanical and the natural ... Machines replaced bodies ... machines overcame nature."[222] It was true. Steam-powered tractors and threshers increased agricultural output. Locomotives pulled

---

221 Bodurtha, *History of Miami County*, 177.
222 White, *Organic Machine*, 30.

loads 365 days a year, not just during the summer. Waterpower was a thing of the past by 1904; new sources of energy eliminated the need for it. The new spatial structure of the town reduced the role of the Wabash River to almost zero in the economic development of the town. The site of the old feeder dam was now the site of the town's new coal-fired electric plant. Discovery of oil and natural gas under the city in 1897 led to a frenzied expansion of industry as many new factories moved into Peru to exploit cheap sources of power and transportation. Industry was free from waterpower; the river was useful only as a tool to remove human and industrial effluent. The Wabash was ignored as anything other than a sewer.

After the 1883 disaster, the Wabash River remained relatively quiet for over two decades, giving the town a respite from major flooding and making it easier for the townspeople to cling to the mistaken notion that the Wabash was irrelevant. The more control that humans applied to the landscape around them, the more they believed that nature was becoming subservient to their power. In reality, each perceived success served only to bind the community more tightly to the natural landscape. Lulled by a false sense of security, Peruvians continued to build homes and businesses in areas vulnerable to a major flood.

Then, in January 1904, the river passed flood stage once again, inundating the town. Heavy rains caused a rapid rise in the river, but the flood fell short of the 1883 level. South Peru, which had grown in size between 1883 and 1904, was pummeled by high water. The flood came and went quickly, causing harm all over the state, but sparing Peru the worst of the damage. Then, in April 1904, the river did something unprecedented; it flooded a second time in the same year. The water level this time missed the 1883 mark by less than a foot. Heavy damage again occurred in South Peru and in the eastern part of Peru. Indiana Manufacturing suffered great damage "with water up to the doorknobs in the buildings" and other factories once more losing thousands of board feet of lumber to the river. [223]

Newspaper accounts from this flood reflect a major change in attitude about the place of the river within the local landscape. This change was due in no small part to the fact that by 1904, Peru had developed a much larger economic base, meaning there was much more to lose. This time the *Peru Republican* explained that the overflow occurred after "The Steady Downpour of Last Friday" and announced "Thousands of Dollars in loss Caused by the Water"; it also acknowledged the suffering of Peru's citizens.[224] It was a far cry from the description given to previous floods. There were no lighthearted stories or references to the forces of nature or acts of God, only a recitation of the losses and failed attempts to divert the water away from South Peru. The paper made no attempt to put a happy face on events. This marks an important shift in the way people interpreted the relationship between the town and the river. A flood was no longer an act of God; it was an unwanted intrusion by nature. Even more importantly, it was an unrestrained force that was out of place in an environment that humans supposedly controlled. Humans needed to find a way to reestablish their dominance in the landscape.

The April 1904 flood was so severe that the water from the Mississinewa pushed across the Wabash, over the recently raised railroad, and up to the foothills in the north, pummeling Peru from that direction as well as from the east. The April 2 edition of the *Peru Daily Chronicle* broached the idea that the town's troubles originated with the overflow of the Mississinewa River, not the Wabash.[225] On April 4, the *Daily Chronicle* estimated total losses at $50,000, with damage concentrated in the eastern and southern parts of town, a pattern of flood damage that remained consistent over the years, with

---

223 *Peru Republican*, April 1, 1904.
224 Ibid.
225 *Peru Daily Chronicle*, April 2, 1904.

the eastern portion of town most vulnerable because of its proximity to the fork of the Wabash and Mississinewa Rivers.[226] As Peru grew in size, the town spread north and west away from the river, but much of the new urban growth was concentrated in a new suburb called Oakdale, less than one-half mile north of the old feeder dam. Over seven hundred plots were laid out there for homes to accommodate the rapid influx of factory workers into Peru. All seven hundred lots sold within three months. The men selling the land ignored the fact that the area was prone to flooding when the Mississinewa pushed north. The floodwater from the 1904 floods was slow to retreat from this district, an unintended consequence of lack of the drainage infrastructure. As a consequence, there was finger-pointing about causes of the flood and arguments among city councilmen about who was responsible "for taking the suburb into the city and then refusing to even consider the question of a remedy for the high water."[227]

The incumbent political and economic leaders of Peru were tasked with solving a difficult problem. Water had long ceased to be the driving force for the economy of the town, but the Wabash River remained, nonetheless. This led to a quandary for town fathers because, despite the destruction caused by floods, Peru continued to grow, making each flood more costly than the last. Factories clung tenaciously to the vicinity of the old feeder dam even though every flood caused severe damage to machinery and inventory. Indiana Manufacturing Company and the Peru Casting Plant were good examples of the refusal of industry to move to a safer location. Both of these businesses added massive complexes along the river after the flood of 1883 and suffered accordingly in 1904.[228] Apparently, the cost of moving was still more than the cost of repairing flood damage because everyone stayed put. Once again, flood stories in the local papers quickly disappeared. There

226 Ibid., April 4, 1904.
227 Ibid., April 2, 4, 5, 1904.
228 Al. D. Beasley, *Twentieth Century Peru* (1901), 64, 125.

were still no easy solutions to the predicament, so the town fathers did what politicians often do when faced with a difficult problem—they ignored it. For the next three years, the local newspapers remained mute on the subject of flood control.

Yet another flood in January 1907 renewed the problem. The *Peru Daily Chronicle* recounted the traditional litany of damages.[229] The *Miami County Sentinel* put no dollar amount to the damages, simply saying it would take "thousands upon thousands of dollars to replace the loss occasioned by the flood" and commenting that most people remembered the lessons of 1904 and were better prepared for the current deluge.[230] Indeed, most people seemed to deal with the river by making an accommodation to the flood. Much of the populace moved carpet and furniture to the second floors of their homes when it became obvious a flood was imminent, but virtually no one evacuated. While they did not have the power to keep the water out, they refused to surrender to the river. They rode the flood out in the upper stories of their houses, and while there were a few close calls, no one died.

This behavior seemed to be a reaffirmation of the pioneer acceptance of the floods as a part of the natural landscape. There was no movement in the community to change the status quo. None of the local papers addressed the economic cost of the flood to the community, but one Indianapolis paper listed two thousand men unemployed, ten factories closed, and damages in excess of $20,000 just during the first day of the flood.[231] Once again, within a week of the flood, the Peru papers stopped making any references to it. There is no detailed list of damage, no guidance on cleanup, and no editorial comment about the need to develop some type of flood control. No city council meetings seriously addressed the problem. Outside of the use of the factory whistle at Indiana Manufacturing as a warning of imminent danger, there was no

---

229 *Peru Daily Chronicle*, January 19, 1907.
230 *Miami County Sentinel*, January 23, 1907.
231 *Indianapolis News*, January 19, 1907.

organized preparation for the flood. After three major floods in three years, the tactic of ignoring the river once again seemed to be a poor strategy, but it is the path the political and economic leaders chose to take.

Industry continued to expand and people continued to build houses in places that now seem absurd. Environmental historians recognize that "when you use and change a landscape, the place will respond. Nature is never passive."[232] However, they have the benefit of hindsight, something the people of Peru lacked. The Wabash River and Peru were originally bound together by the canal. The bond could be altered, but not severed. As the town grew and technology changed, the relationship between the river and the town became more complicated. By the time Peruvians began to understand just how intertwined their lives were with the river, it was too late to avoid a major disaster.

After 1907, the people of Peru assumed they had seen the worst floods that the Wabash River had to offer, but in March 1913, events took place that altered perceptions about the relationship between the town and river forever. Economic growth had continued after the 1907 flood. By 1913, the town boasted a population of roughly thirteen thousand citizens as well as a rapidly growing industrial base.[233] The industrial center of the town continued to shift northward away from the river into Oakdale. Other than an attempt to lessen flooding in South Peru by raising Riverside Drive about three feet to create a dike, the city had done nothing since 1907 to alleviate ongoing problems caused by the river. Some of the residents of South Peru also raised their homes two or three feet in the hope that they could avoid future flood damage, but those were individual actions, not because of city planning.

---

232 William Deverell and Greg Hise, eds., *Land of Sunshine: An Environmental History of Metropolitan Los Angeles* (Pittsburgh: University of Pittsburgh Press, 2005), 224.

233 Bodurtha, *History of Miami County*, 177.

For the most part, there was no organized effort to deal with the flood problem, with one exception. Peru's largest factory was still the Indiana Manufacturing Company, the only major industry other than the railroad that remained along the river. The manager of the company, Elbert W. Shirk, knew that the raised railroad embankment to the southeast of the factory magnified flood problems for his factory and the town.

Elbert W. Shirk
(Photo courtesy of the Miami County, Indiana, Historical Society)

For years he tried to get the city to address the problems caused by the river, but city leaders ignored his advice.[234] On Saturday, March 22, 1913, Shirk's fears became a reality, and the people of Peru learned a grim lesson about the power of the Wabash River.

---

234 *Peru Republican*, April 4, 1913.

The 1913 flood was unlike any other flood in the history of Peru. The ground around Peru was soaked from previous storms, and the river was already high as the Easter weekend rain began on the twenty-second. Over the next five days, almost eight inches of rain and snow fell on the water-soaked upper Wabash Valley, overwhelming the capacity of the ground to absorb any further moisture.[235] The massive amount of drainage tile did its job and funneled hundreds of millions of gallons of water into the swollen Wabash River. Water data from the United States Geologic Service states that the normal amount of stream flow for the Wabash River at Peru in 1913 was around 10,000 cubic feet per second (CFS). The major floods experienced in the town before 1913 averaged 20,000 to 30,000 CFS. The 1913 flood dwarfed those numbers, peaking at a staggering 118,000 CFS, almost seven times worse than any previous flood.[236] Decades of deforestation, ditching, tiling, and other destabilizing ecological practices contributed to what has been described as a five-hundred-year event.[237] The environmental shotgun that was aimed at the city of Peru went off with a big bang.

The weather in Peru turned bad on Good Friday with high winds and rain and snow mixing at times. Many churches cancelled Easter services on Sunday because of torrential rains, and by Monday morning, Peruvians realized that the river was going to overflow its banks. Elbert Shirk had eyed the river nervously for years and knew the Indiana Manufacturing Company complex was vulnerable to flooding. He tried to divert the water away from the 1.5 million board feet of lumber stacked alongside the factory by organizing his workers into a makeshift dam-building crew. On Monday, they built a temporary wall across Canal Street in an

235 Jehu Z. Powell, *History of Cass County, Indiana* (Chicago: Lewis Publishing, 1913), 303–7.

236 United States Department of the Interior, *USGS 03327500 Wabash River at Peru, In.* <http://nwis.waterdata.usgs.gov/in/nwis/peak/?site_no=03327500&>, April 2, 2009.

237 US Army Corps of Engineers, *Indianapolis North Flood Damage Reduction Project No. Ld-11-084. Project Data* (Louisville, KY, 2007), 3.

attempt to protect the plant. They succeeded in stopping seven feet of water from pushing through, but by Monday afternoon Shirk saw that water would soon overwhelm the dike, and he ordered it abandoned.[238]

Shirk's experience reveals the scale of the 1913 flood. Indiana Manufacturing had been flooded numerous times in the past, but the company always overcame the financial losses. This time was different. Shirk, a Harvard-educated businessman who understood the potential danger of a flood and tried to prepare for it, was completely overwhelmed by the scale of the catastrophe. He spent the wee hours of Monday morning standing in icy cold water trying to save valuable papers inside his office. By the time he gave up, the water was almost up to his shoulders. By late Monday night, the rising water swept his factory from end to end, washing away the lumber.[239] Much of the lumber that washed away from the factory snagged on the trusses of the new cement bridge just a short distance downstream from the plant at Wayne Street. This had the effect of creating a massive dam across the Wabash and diverted even more water directly into the streets of Peru. In one last attempt to save the business, Shirk, at great risk to his life, spent much of Thursday trying to fasten some of the great piles of lumber together in order to save them. Despite his efforts, most of the lumber was ruined, swept downstream, or pilfered by locals to use in rebuilding after the flood was over.[240]

Legend has it that quite a few houses were repaired after the flood using lumber scavenged from along the banks of the Wabash. Shirk's losses amounted to about $250,000, a huge sum by 1913 standards.[241] Indiana Manufacturing could not absorb the loss and finally went out of business, ending the major industrial presence along the old canal once and for all.

---

238 *Peru Republican*, April 4, 1913.
239 Ibid.
240 Ibid.
241 Bodurtha, *History of Miami County*, 406.

Indiana Manufacturing after the 1913 flood.
Note the high-water marks on the building.
(Photo courtesy of the Miami County, Indiana, Historical Society)

Monday afternoon, while Shirk and his men were waging their battle on Canal Street, people near the river took the normal course of action, pulling up carpet and moving furniture to the second stories of their houses. There was no panic or undue concern over the situation, especially by the people who lived on the high side of town north of the river. It was rare for water to be more than a nuisance there. South Peru was another matter. Despite the recent elevation of Riverside Drive, the land south of the city was still vulnerable to flooding along the low-lying streets. By Monday afternoon, storm sewers in the streets south of the river were spewing water. Unlike some of the bigger cities affected by the 1913 flood, such as Dayton, Ohio, there was no kind of warning system in place to broadcast the severity of the flood, nor was there an organized plan to warn people of the danger.[242] Consequently, most residents anticipated a typical flood, one that brought two or three feet of water down the streets, resulting in a few hours of isolation in their houses. Few people contemplated evacuation.[243]

The rapid rise of the river was unexpected because no previous flood ever hit so quickly. Early reports from towns upriver indicated a

---

242 US Army Corps of Engineers, *Indianapolis North Flood Damage*, 2.
243 *Peru Republican*, April 4, 1913.

flood similar to those in the past, but by six o'clock in the evening, the floodwaters exploded over the riverbank east of town and began flowing into the low areas of South Peru. In less than an hour, the water was knee high, and many people decided to head for the hills south of town, while others complacently made the decision to ride out the flood in their homes. As a windy, bitterly cold night fell, more and more citizens of South Peru decided to head for high ground, but the rising water and the fast-moving current soon ended the evacuation efforts.[244]

There was unease on the north side of the Wabash also. Grocery stores did a brisk business as people stocked up on food, candles, and other necessities. At eight o'clock in the evening, the town fire whistle began to shriek. Omer Holman, editor of the *Peru Republican*, explained the reason for the warning:

As it sounded longer and louder than usual, I went to Broadway to ascertain the location of the fire. I soon learned that the whistle was the signal that the city water was to be turned off as there was danger of the river getting into the water works station real soon. I hurried home and filled every empty vessel in the house with water. I did not neglect filling the tub, either.[245]

Earlier on Monday, the *Peru Evening Journal* rushed an issue to press warning of a possible flood, but with only a mention that it might be comparable to 1907.[246] Hundreds of curiosity seekers lined the banks of the Wabash at the foot of Broadway to watch the water creep higher. While Elbert Shirk was frantically trying to divert the flood away from his furniture factory, many of the town's citizens, oblivious to the danger, flocked to South Broadway to gawk. Complacency dissolved by Monday afternoon as the river began to rise at the alarming rate of eight to twelve inches an hour. Those who lived near the river braced for the flood, but many people on the north side of the river had no idea how

244 *Peru Evening Journal*, March 24, 1913.
245 *Peru Republican*, April 4, 1913.
246 *Peru Evening Journal*, March 24, 1913.

fast the water was rising. Until the fire siren went off at 8:00 p.m., most of them believed there was no reason for concern.

Another man alarmed by the situation was Colonel Ben Wallace, owner of the circus that was in winter quarters just east of town.

Ben Wallace
(Photo courtesy of the Miami County, Indiana, Historical Society)

He was not prepared for a flood. Hundreds of exotic animals were in danger at his farm, which was already flooding. The circus had many big cats, elephants, hippos, and polar bears at the farm, not to mention hundreds of head of livestock and other animals. Because the farm was less than a mile above the confluence of the Wabash and Mississinewa Rivers, it was one of the first places cut off, and Wallace, who was at his home in Peru, was unable to get there. When a reporter from the *Peru Republican* asked Wallace if there was any news, he answered, "I would not be surprised to learn that the whole show property is washed into the Mississinewa River, and that the seventy-five men, as well as all my animals and horses, are dead."[247] His concerns were valid. The loss to the circus was horrendous. Besides the death of many valuable animals, including four elephants and all of the big cats, most of the tents, circus wagons, train cars, and other equipment needed to run the show suffered damage. The monetary loss to Wallace was over $150,000. He could not absorb such a huge loss and sold the circus four months later.[248]

Things were dangerous north of the river also. The ground sloped gently upward the farther away one got from the river, but by Tuesday morning, water levels along both Canal and Second Streets reached ten feet in places. Part of the reason for this was the giant logjam at the concrete bridge on Wayne Street.[249] As the lumber from the Peru Manufacturing Company floated downstream Monday night and wedged against the bridge, the floodwater surged around the obstruction and into the streets of Peru. By Tuesday afternoon, pummeled by the current and debris, the Broadway Bridge washed away. Many people headed for the taller buildings downtown or for higher ground at the east end of town. Hundreds of refugees on the east side ended up marooned on a rise that came to be known as Smith's Island. There was so little shelter there that over one hundred people were forced to cram into one small five-room house. They packed the place so completely that there was no room for anyone to sit down. Many wet and tired victims stood for the entire night.

Men in boats braved the dangers of the current and floating debris to pluck people from windows, trees, and roofs. All over town, people scrambled to gather family members, move furniture and carpeting upstairs, and provide for the safety of livestock. There were many instances of cows and horses being brought onto porches or even into houses in order to get them out of the weather and give them a chance

247 Ibid.
248 Bodurtha, *History of Miami County*, 406.
249 *Peru Republican*, April 4, 1913.

to survive. Some of the livestock served a more immediate purpose. "The first night, we saw our chicken in the coop was going to drown, so Clevinger waded out and got it ... we had stewed hen Tuesday evening for supper."[250] Untold numbers of animals drowned or died from exposure.

Looking north from the ridge in South Peru
(Photo courtesy of the author)

As the rescue boats made their rounds, the number of residents congregating on high ground grew. Smith's Island ended up with over twelve hundred people trying to find shelter in only eighteen houses. In Oakdale, over a thousand people stayed at the Booth factory while another two hundred jammed into Elmwood School. Other refugees found shelter with friends, family, or strangers who were fortunate enough to live in areas above the flood. In the western part of town, the high school, along with the Holman Street School and the Lutheran School, became refugee centers. An estimated three thousand individuals huddled at the courthouse and in the upper levels of other downtown buildings. When boats weren't rescuing people, they were ferrying supplies from the ridges north and south of town to relief centers scattered about on high ground.

250 "Letter from Sylvia to Joe," Miami County Historical Society (1913).

The newspaper accounts of the 1913 flood were far different than any previous flood. No longer would anyone put marks on walls to remember what happened. The balance sheet now was marked by the human toll. Delight Shields was a seventeen-year-old young woman who worked as a secretary in Peru. She lived in South Peru, along with her mother. They were unable to escape the flood before the rising water made it impossible to walk out. During the attempt to rescue them, the raft on which they rode was caught by the current and slammed into the porch of a home on Franklin Street, dashing it to pieces. Everyone but Delight was able to grab onto something solid, but she vanished in the swiftly moving water. Her body was found a week later over two miles downstream from the accident scene.

One man drowned at the northern edge of town, and two railroad workers died when the current pulled their boat out from under them as they tried to run a wire across the Wabash so boats could be ferried from one side to the other. The bodies of a man named Gintner and his daughter were found in the old canal bed not far from the concrete bridge, and another was found sitting on an overturned china cabinet in one of the houses.[251]

On the south side of the river, the rescuers concentrated on getting people to the ridge that ran along the edge of town. The flood victims were transferred by wagon to rural homes for refuge, or by rail to towns such as Amboy and Converse, where food and shelter were provided by the local citizenry. The rescue work was dangerous because the area was lower than the river, and in many places the water was fifteen to twenty feet deep. In addition, wreckage floating downstream hindered the effort.[252]

---

251 *Peru Republican*, April 11, 1913.
252 *Peru Evening Journal*, March 31, 1913.

Wreckage of homes in South Peru
(Photo courtesy of the Miami County, Indiana, Historical Society)

All day Tuesday, men such as Roma B. Mays paddled through the rain and snow that was still falling, pulling victims through second-story windows, plucking them from rooftops, and nosing into treetops so half-frozen survivors could jump into the dubious safety of the small boats. One South Peru woman wrote of that Tuesday, "It was so distressing. We could hear people calling for help and all night long they kept it up. Cloe [sic] and I kept watch that night and we could just hear so many voices calling for help."[253] Officials later estimated that Mays alone brought over two hundred individuals to safety.[254] At some point, late in the day on Tuesday, he was bringing another group of people to safety when his luck ran out. One of the passengers in the boat panicked, throwing everyone into the water. Mays might have saved himself, but he tried to help the woman who had upset the boat, and both drowned. Townspeople later hailed him as one of the biggest heroes of the flood.[255]

Never before had the river caused such chaos. Peru had never experienced flood-related deaths before, and it was a miracle that only eleven people drowned during the 1913 flood. The final death toll was

253 Ibid.
254 Ibid.
255 Ibid.

higher because of residents who later succumbed to flood-related sickness. Over the weeks immediately following the flood, a significant number of obituaries in the Peru papers referred to exposure as a contributing factor of death. Many of these people were elderly, so it is impossible to determine to what extent their deaths were directly attributable to the flood, but it would be fair to say that the final death toll from the disaster was between twenty and twenty-five.

The consequences for Peru were immediate and long-lasting. Owners abandoned many of the damaged or destroyed buildings along the waterfront. The seven-acre Indiana Manufacturing complex never recovered. Elbert Shirk moved the business to Richmond, Indiana, taking away five hundred jobs. Industrial growth stagnated; no other major manufacturer built in Peru until after the end of World War II. The population of the town never again exceeded that of 1913. The damage to the infrastructure of Peru was massive, and South Peru was shattered. Only a handful of houses survived. One-third of the homes in the rest of Peru were ruined, and another third suffered damage.[256]

South Peru after the flood
(Photo courtesy of the Miami County, Indiana, Historical Society)

256 Bodurtha, *History of Miami County*, 406.

Two of the town's three bridges were swept away, and every business within three blocks of the river sustained large losses. Some of them never reopened. Many of the factories in Oakdale also were damaged. Material losses to Peru amounted to a staggering $2,000,000 in 1913 dollars.[257] That number does not include lost production or the cost to the community of the permanent closure of factories and businesses. The scale of the disaster dwarfed anything that had ever happened before, making the traditional response to flooding irrelevant. Ignoring the problem was no longer an option. In one fell swoop, the disaster exposed decades of misunderstanding and denial about the power and place of the Wabash River in the life of the town.

The traditional view of nature separated humans from the environment, but the flood revealed just how thin the line was. The damage forced the citizens of Peru to reevaluate the question of where the river fit within the landscape, reminding them that despite their efforts to minimize the importance of the river, it was still the center of the landscape, dominating the economic fortunes of the town and making itself impossible to ignore. Peruvians had looked beyond water for their economic future, while remaining oblivious to the fact that the very progress they sought altered the river, making them increasingly vulnerable to the increasingly unstable Wabash. It was one thing to abandon the canal; abandoning the river was not so easy.

Local industrial and governmental leaders realized they could no longer afford to dismiss the power of the river. They asked questions echoed years later by environmental historian Marc Reisner: "Where do we place ourselves in nature? Are we the masters of the environment or merely players within it?"[258] Peruvians reacted to their epiphany by pressing for literal control of the river in the form of dams. One civic leader declared that without the dams, "Peru cannot hope to attract

---

257 Ibid.
258 Marc Reisner. *Cadillac Desert: The American West and Its Disappearing Water* (New York: Viking, 1986), 497.

major industries, to see fine homes erected, or to draw to this center wealth which is essential to our cities' prosperity."[259] It was a far cry from the days when the Peru paper bragged that the city could, if necessary, "live perfectly independent of the rest of the world, were we surrounded by a Chinese wall."[260] The boast about surrounding Peru with a wall had changed to a plea for help. The line between what was human and what was natural was blurred by the 1913 flood. Peru needed a way to refocus it, and what clearer line was there than a dam?

Up until 1913, any effort to address flooding was done at the local level, but soon after the flood, Indiana established four regional flood districts to tackle the problem. One of those districts was in Peru.[261] The move marked a dramatic shift as state and federal entities assumed the bulk of responsibility for flood control. This was both good and bad for Peru. It was good because it brought new engineering resources into the discussion and planning, but it was bad because the state and federal government did not always pay for the plans they formulated. Even worse, federal involvement with its accompanying red tape slowed action to a crawl.

The residents of Peru got their first dose of this new reality soon after the 1913 flood ended. The town's main bridge across the Wabash River washed out during the flood. While making plans to replace it quickly, local planners were shocked when they learned that in the interest of national security, Congress and the War Department had to approve any new structure.[262] Although the bridge could have been replaced within three or four months, it took eight months before federal approval was gained when Congress passed H.R. 8702, the bill authorizing the city of Peru to "construct, maintain, and operate a bridge and approaches

---

259 *Miami County Sentinel*, June 26, 1943.
260 Ibid., July 27, 1848.
261 *American Political Science Review* IX, no. 1 (1915): 752–53.
262 *Miami County Sentinel*, August 13, 1913.

thereto across the Wabash River."[263] The legislation provided no funding for the project. Construction of the new bridge did not begin until almost a year after the flood. The federal government was quick to assume control of the problem but slow to finance a solution. It was a portent of things to come.

The consensus of expert opinion after March 1913 was that future protection along the Wabash River depended not only on dams and levees, but also on reforestation, an acknowledgment that human manipulation of the landscape played a role in the flooding.[264] The Army Corps of Engineers also visited Peru in May 1913 to study the river and formulate a flood prevention plan.[265] The group of engineers decided the answer to Peru's dilemma was a levee. The plan called for raising the height of all bridges, dredging the river to remove obstructions, clearing the riverbank of all trees and brush, and the construction of a twelve-foot-high earthen wall along the north side of the Wabash River that would extend from one end of town to the other.[266] Engineers considered this a stopgap measure until they could conduct thorough surveys along the upper Wabash Valley and formulate permanent flood control plans.[267] The plan was expensive and was received with little enthusiasm by city leaders, who preferred the building of a dam on the Wabash. They wanted to control the water on a larger scale. The only part of the levee ever built was at the east end of town, and it had little impact on flood prevention.

The 1913 flood was the catalyst for Peru as well as other towns along the Wabash to organize and make long-term plans for flood control.

---

263 Congress, An Act to Authorize the County of Miami, Indiana to Construct a Bridge across the Wabash River in Miami, County, H.R. 8702, November 27, 1913.

264 Robert M. Brown, "The Ohio River Floods of 1913," *Bulletin of the American Geographical Society* 45, no. 7 (1913): 508.

265 *Peru Republican*, May 22, 1913.

266 *Miami County Sentinel*, January 14, 1914.

267 Ibid.

These efforts began soon after the 1913 flood when a delegation of civic leaders from Peru appeared before the Indiana Railroad Commission to make the argument that the severity of the flood was magnified by the elevated grade of the railroad that ran along the river.[268] This was the first official acknowledgment by Peruvians that human interference in the environment played a significant role in the flooding of the town. Over the next thirty years, as the semiannual floods continued, state and federal officials commiserated with the cities along the Upper Wabash but made little progress in solving the problem.

There was not another catastrophic flood until 1943. It marked a regional shift in thinking about the problem. The city governments of every town along the upper Wabash Valley from Huntington to Delphi acknowledged the need for help when they met to form a flood prevention association, which would lobby the federal government for financial aid.[269]

The effort to establish a flood control district along the Wabash River did not gain any momentum until after the end of World War II, but by 1958, the federal government finally approved almost $50,000,000 for a series of three dams along the Wabash and its tributaries.[270] One dam would be built on the Wabash River at Huntington, one on the Salamonie River at Wabash, and one on the Mississinewa River at Peru (see Figure 9).

---

268 *Peru Evening Journal*, May 12, 1913.
269 *Miami County Sentinel*, June 26, 1943.
270 US Senate, Flood Control Act of 1958.

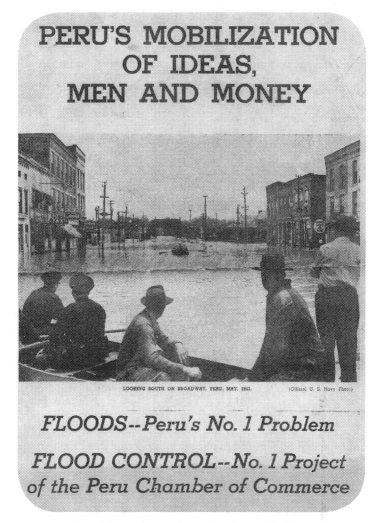

PERU'S MOBILIZATION OF IDEAS, MEN AND MONEY

LOOKING SOUTH ON BROADWAY, PERU, MAY, 1943.   (Official U. S. Navy Photo)

FLOODS--Peru's No. 1 Problem

FLOOD CONTROL--No. 1 Project
of the Peru Chamber of Commerce

Pamphlet used to promote flood control efforts
(Photo courtesy of the Miami County, Indiana, Historical Society)

On April 27, 1962, exactly forty-nine years and one month after the peak of the 1913 flood, the Army Corps of Engineers broke ground on the Mississinewa dam project. By 1967, it was completed, marking an end to the three-dam project and ushering in a new vision of human protection and control along the upper Wabash Valley.[271] Protection,

---

271   *Peru Daily Tribune*, May 27, 1982.

however, does not necessarily equal control. The last flood to hit Peru was in 1959. Since then, the river has been relatively quiet because of the dams, but not inactive. In 1999, the Army Corps of Engineers realized that the Mississinewa dam, an earthen structure, seemed to be shifting. Testing revealed that water had infiltrated the base of the structure and found its way through to the other side.[272] It took forty years, but the Mississinewa River had found a way to overcome human technology and reassert itself within the landscape. Engineers had to drain most of the water out of the reservoir, drill down to bedrock, and install a wall within one side of the dam to stop further erosion. The repairs began in January 2002, lasted until the spring of 2005, and cost $55,000,000.[273] The relationship between humans and the rivers of the upper Wabash Valley continues to shift, but it is far from over.

The misperception of the human place within the natural landscape is the catalyst for much of the history surrounding the town of Peru. Looking at that history from an environmental perspective offers a new layer in the area's historical record. Humans introduced both themselves and their technology into the local landscape with the mistaken assumption that they could control and manipulate both the land and water of the region for their economic benefit.

Nowhere was the effect of this miscalculation more evident than in the increasingly erratic behavior of the Wabash River at Peru. As a result of the environmental changes brought about by people, the economic advantages offered by the location of Peru slowly disappeared under the steady assault of the Wabash River. The power of water was the reason Peru was built and also was the main reason why the town saw its economic fortunes decline after 1913.

272 *Peru Daily Tribune*, February 19, 2001.
273 Fact Sheet: *Mississinewa Dam Safety Project* (US Army Corps of Engineers, 2004).

CHAPTER 4

Consequences

THE CONNECTION BETWEEN PERU AND THE WABASH RIVER IS A tangled landscape created through the interaction of humans and nature. The first humans to live and work along the river left a small environmental footprint, living in harmony with the landscape. It was not until the introduction of American settlers to the region that the relationship changed. Men like Joseph Holman and William Hood believed they could change the upper Wabash Valley to fit their own economic and cultural visions. The relationship that developed created a new landscape, one in which humans sought control over the most powerful natural feature in northern Indiana, the Wabash River. Starting with the construction of the Wabash & Erie Canal, people spent the next eighty years building, digging, and draining along the river, while failing to see that interaction with the environment was changing the behavior of the river. It was not until the Wabash River destroyed much of Peru that people began to seriously question their place within the landscape of the upper Wabash Valley.

There are often unexpected consequences when humans attempt to alter nature. No matter what we do to nature, it always responds. No matter how dominant human technology seems to be, nature always seeks balance. The line between man-made and natural is often blurred to the point where it is no longer relevant. No matter how hard people try to change the landscape, nature has a way of altering the new environment, often in ways that make it even stronger than before.[274] The same process occurred along the Wabash River.

Misconceptions about the role of people and nature led to decisions about the use of water that defined the history of Peru, Indiana, and the region around it. The Wabash & Erie Canal brought both economic growth and environmental chaos to the area. The decision to build Peru in a vulnerable location so close to the fork of the Wabash and Mississinewa Rivers was based solely on economic advantages created by the canal. The canal brought thousands of settlers to Miami County. They introduced man-made improvements that altered the natural environment in various ways, creating a new landscape in the process.

The new agricultural economy around Peru as well as the industry within the town depended on the assumption that human technology was superior to the power of nature. They did not understand the ability of nature to adapt to man-made alterations to the landscape. That lack of understanding caused the operation of the canal to be more complicated and expensive than anticipated. Banks collapsed, weeds clogged the water, and weather damaged locks and viaducts. For every move people made to overcome natural obstacles, nature adapted.

Man dug, drained, and elevated the landscape around Peru in an effort to gain the upper hand over nature, but technology did not always equal control; it often led to unpredictable consequences when nature pushed back. The ultimate reaction to the changes humans brought to the landscape was flooding. The history of Peru shows an escalating pattern of environmental interaction between humans and the river. The more people tampered with the land, the more severe the flooding became.

---

274 Fiege, *Irrigated Eden*, 9.

The idea of Manifest Destiny promoted the idea that man was separated from nature by technology, when in fact the line along the Wabash River was being blurred by human interaction. It wasn't until the Wabash River erased the line completely in 1913 that the residents of Peru realized how connected they were with the river. What was natural had combined with what was man-made to create something Peruvians needed but could not control. They spent nearly another century seeking ways to regain control over their environment. The solution they arrived at was to dam the river that defied them. As of 2012, the battle seems to have swung in their favor, but as the repairs to the Mississinewa dam show, nature is patient and relentless in its work. The remains of one of the greatest engineering feats of the nineteenth century, the Wabash & Erie Canal, also attest to the inevitable marriage between human endeavor and the power of nature.

The Wabash & Erie Canal at the east edge of Peru in 2012
(Photo courtesy of the author)

Environmental history writers have developed the idea that nature is inseparable from humanity. Historians have looked at the theme of water and nature in particular to show how the relationship between people and rivers intertwine. Environmental history has evolved from the assumption that nature is an expansive, pristine place disconnected from humanity to the notion that it is a partner and is integral to our environmental landscape. Rivers play a large part in that progression of historical thought. William Cronon, one of the best writers in the field of environmental history, has said that we need to find some kind of middle ground in which a common definition applies to the landscape that enfolds us. He uses the term "home" because it is "the place we try to sustain so we can pass along what is best in it (and ourselves) to our children."[275]

The historical lesson that the story of the Wabash River and Peru, Indiana, teaches is that home is a landscape created by a combination of what is man-made and what is natural. On that day so long ago when I stood on my kitchen stoop and watched the water from the Wabash River lap at the foundation of our house, I made the same mistake that so many people make about the landscape in which we live. I thought the town and the river were separate things. They weren't. They defined my home. The riverfront wasn't necessarily a dumb place to put a house; it was a *natural* place to build because of the relationship between the people of Peru and the Wabash River. When it comes to understanding the meaning of home, the history of Peru shows that the Wabash River still has lessons to impart in Nature's School.

---

275 William Cronon, "The Trouble with Wilderness," 24.

Bibliography

Primary Sources

Beasley, Al. D. *Twentieth Century Peru*. Peru, 1901.

Bert, Joseph Griswold, and Samuel R. Taylor. *The Pictorial History of Fort Wayne, Indiana: A Review of Two Centuries of Occupation of the Region About the Head of the Maumee River*. Chicago: Robert O. Law, 1917.

Biographical and Genealogical History of Cass, Miami, Howard, and Tipton Counties, Indiana. 2 vols. Vol. 1. Chicago: Lewis Publishing, 1898.

Bodurtha, Arthur L. *History of Miami County: A Narrative Account of Its Historical Progress, Its People, and Its Principal Interests*. Vol. 1. Chicago: Lewis Publishing, 1914.

Brown, Robert M. "The Ohio River Floods of 1913." *Bulletin of the American Geographical Society* 45, no. 7 (1913): 500–509.

City Directory of Peru 1886–1887. Logansport, Indiana: Hall and O'Donald, 1887.

Collections of the Kansas State Historical Society. Edited by George W. Martin. Vol. XII. Topeka: State Printing Office, 1912.

Dillon, John Brown. *A History of Indiana from Its Earliest Exploration by Europeans*. Indianapolis: Bingham and Doughty, 1859.

Dresser, Paul. *On the Banks of the Wabash, Far Away*. New York: Howley, Haviland, 1897.

Dryer, Charles Redway. "The Maumee-Wabash Waterway." *Annals of the Association of American Geographers* 9 (1919): 41–51.

Early Western Travels, 1748–1846. Edited by Reuben Gold Thwaites. 32 vols. Cleveland: Arthur H. Clark, 1904–1907.

Fort Wayne (IN) Sentinel.

Gatschet, Albert S. "Water-Monsters of the American Aborigines." *Journal of American Folklore* 12, no. 47 (1899): 255–60.

Godfroy, Chief Clarence. *Miami Indian Stories*. Winona Lake, IN: Light and Life Press, 1961.

Government, United States. *Indian Affairs: Laws and Treaties*. Edited by Charles J. Kappler. Vol. II. Washington DC: Government Printing Office, 1904.

Graham, John. *Pioneer History of Peru and Miami County*. Peru, IN: Peru Republican Printing Office, 1877.

History of Cass County Indiana. Edited by Dr. Jehu Z. Powell. Chicago: Lewis Publishing, 1913.

History of Miami County Indiana. Edited by Brant and Fuller. Chicago: Brant and Fuller, 1887.

Holman, Omer. *Peru Pictures Past and Present*. Peru, IN: Peru Republican Printing Office, 1909.

———. *Here We Live Over the Last Fifty Years*. Peru, IN: Peru Republican Printing Office, 1935.

Hundley, Will M. *Squawtown: My Boyhood Among the Last Miami Indians*. Caldwell, ID: Caxton Printers, 1939.

Indiana Department of Geology and Natural Resources, Indiana Geological Survey. "36th Annual Report of Department of Geology and Natural Resources, Indiana." Edited by Indiana Department of Geology and Natural Resources, 796. Indianapolis, 1911.

Indianapolis (IN) News.

Kettleborough, Charles. *Drainage and Reclamation of Swamp and Overflowed Lands: Indiana Bureau of Legislative Information, Bulletin No. 2*, Indianapolis: State of Indiana, 1914.

Leverett, Frank. *Water Resources of Indiana and Ohio.* Edited by Department of the Interior US Geological Survey. Vol. IV. Washington DC: Government Printing Office, 1897.

"Letter from Sylvia to Joe." Miami County Historical Society, 1913.

Logansport (IN) Canal Telegraph.

Lonn, Ella. "Life and Journal of John Sutherland." *Mississippi Valley Historical Review* 4, no. 3 (1917): 362–70.

Miami County Recorder. *Plat of Mill Lots at Peru*, Book 1, 584, 1851.

Miami County (IN) Sentinel.

Peru (IN) Daily Chronicle.

Peru (IN) Daily Tribune.

Peru (IN) Evening Journal.

Peru (IN) Forester.

Peru (IN) Observer.

Peru (IN) Republican.

Raymond, William Galt. *The Elements of Railroad Engineering.* New York: John Wiley & Sons, 1914.

Representatives, Indiana House of. "Select Committee of the House of Representatives in the Case of Jesse L. Williams, Principal Engineer, January 4, 1836." (No page numbers), *Documentary Journal* (1836).

Service, National Weather. "Advanced Hydrologic Prediction Service." Edited by NOAA, 2009.

Stephens, John H. *History of Miami County: Illustrated*. Peru, IN: John H. Stephens Publishing, 1896.

Stuart, Charles B. *Lives and Works of Civil and Military Engineers of America*. New York: D. Van Nostrand, 1871.

US Congress. Senate. *Act to Authorize the County of Miami, Indiana to Construct a Bridge across the Wabash River in Miami, County*. Session I, Ch. 38 and 39: 1914.

US Congress. Senate. *Flood Control Act of 1958*.

US Army Corps of Engineers. *Fact Sheet: Mississinewa Dam Safety Project*, 1: 2004.

———. "Indianapolis North Flood Damage Reduction Project No. Ld-11-084 Project Data." 4. Louisville, 2007.

———. United States Mississippi River Commission. *Annual Report of the Chief of Engineers U.S. Army*. III vols. Vol. III: US Government Printing Office, 1881.

Weaver, Clarence E. *A Description of the City of Peru, Miami County, Indiana*. Peru, IN: The Indiana Advancement Company, 1897.

Williams, Jesse L. "Wabash & Erie Canal 1847 Chief Engineers Report on Structures." 1847.

Woollen, William Wesley, Daniel Wait Howe, Jacob Piatt Dunn. "Executive Journal of Indiana Territory, 1800–1816." *Indiana Historical Society Publications* III, no. III (1900): 252.

Young, Andrew W. *History of Wayne County, Indiana: From Its First Settlement to the Present Time*. Cincinnati: Robert Clarke, 1872.

Secondary Sources

American Political Science Review IX, no. 1 (1915): 752–53.

Bemis, Samuel Flagg. *Jay's Treaty: A Study in Commerce and Diplomacy.* New Haven, CT: Yale University Press, 1962.

Benke, Arthur C., and Colbert E. Cushing. *Rivers of North America: The Natural History.* Burlington, MA: Academic Press, 2005.

Blackford, Glen A. *The John Tipton Papers.* Edited by Dorothy Riker and Nellie Armstrong Robertson. 3 vols. Vol. I. Indianapolis: Indiana Historical Bureau, 1942.

Coppernoll, Marilyn. *Miami County, Indiana: A Pictorial History.* Virginia Beach: Donning, 1995.

Carter, Harvey L. "Rural Indiana in Transition, 1850–1860." *Agricultural History* 20, no. 2 (1946): 107–21.

Castaldi, Thomas E. *Wabash & Erie Canal Notebook I: Allen and Huntington Counties.* 2nd ed. Fort Wayne, IN: Parrot Printing, 2002.

———. *Wabash & Erie Canal Notebook II: Wabash and Miami Counties.* Fort Wayne, IN: Parrot Printing, 2004.

Cronon, William. *Nature's Metropolis: Chicago and the Great West.* New York: W. W. Norton, 1991.

———. "The Trouble with Wilderness or, Getting Back to the Wrong Nature." *Environmental History* 1, no. 1 (1996): 7–28.

Fatout, Paul. *Indiana Canals.* West Lafayette, IN: Purdue University Press, 1972.

Fiege, Mark. *Irrigated Eden: The Making of an Agricultural Landscape in the American West.* Seattle: University of Washington Press, 1999.

Gammon, James R. *The Wabash River Ecosystem.* Bloomington: Indiana University Press, 1998.

Hays, Samuel P. *Conservation and the Gospel of Efficiency.* Cambridge, MA: Harvard University Press, 1959.

Hick, Ronald. *The Hidden Community: The Miami Indians of Indiana, 1846–1940.* Muncie, IN: Ball State University, 1992.

Indiana Historian, 1993: 1–16.

Jackson, Kenneth T. *Crabgrass Frontier: The Suburbanization of the United States.* New York: Oxford University Press, 1985.

Kelman, Ari. *A River and Its City: The Nature of Landscape in New Orleans.* Berkeley: University of California Press, 2006.

Lamb, E. Wendell, Josephine Lamb, and Lawrence Shultz. *More Indian Lore.* Winona Lake, IN: Light and Life Press, 1968.

Land of Sunshine: An Environmental History of Metropolitan Los Angeles. Edited by William Deverell and Greg Hise, 220–44. Pittsburgh: University of Pittsburgh Press, 2005.

Lindsey, Alton A., Robert O. Petty, David K. Sterling, and Willard Van Asdall. "Vegetation and Environment along the Wabash and Tippecanoe Rivers." *Ecological Monographs* 31, no. 2 (1961): 105–56.

Lindsey, Alton A. "Vegetation of the Drainage-Aeration Classes of Northern Indiana Soils in 1830." *Ecology* 42, no. 2 (1961): 432–36.

Mann, Rob. "The Silenced Miami: Archaeological and Ethnohistorical Evidence for Miami-British Relations, 1795–1812." *Ethnohistory* 46, no. 3 (1999): 399–427.

Meyer, David R. "Midwestern Industrialization and the American Manufacturing Belt in the Nineteenth Century." *Journal of Economic History* 49, no. 4 (1989): 921–37.

Moriarty, J. T. *Manifest Destiny: A Primary Source History of America's Territorial Expansion in the 19th Century.* New York: Rosen Publishing, 2005.

O'Sullivan, John. "The Great Nation of Futurity." *The United States Democratic Review* 6, no. 23 (1839): 426–30.

Palmer, Tim. *The Snake River: Window to the West.* Washington DC: Island Press, 1991.

Pisani, Donald J. "Beyond the Hundredth Meridian: Nationalizing the History of Water in the United States." *Environmental History* 5, no. 4 (2000): 466–82.

Poinsatte, Charles R. *Fort Wayne during the Canal Era: 1828–1855.* Indianapolis: Indiana Historical Bureau, 1969.

Rae, John Bell. "Federal Land Grants in Aid of Canals." *Journal of Economic History* 4, no. 2 (1944): 167–77.

Rafert, Stewart. *The Miami Indians of Indiana; a Persistent People.* Indianapolis: Indiana Historical Society Press, 1996.

Reisner, Marc. *Cadillac Desert: The American West and Its Disappearing Water.* New York: Viking, 1986.

Scheiber, Harry N. "Entrepreneurship and Western Development: The Case of Micajah T. Williams." *Business History Review* 37, no. 4 (1963): 345–68.

———."State Policy and the Public Domain: The Ohio Canal Lands." *Journal of Economic History* 25, no. 1 (1965): 86–113.

Setzler, Frank M. *The Archaeology of the Whitewater Valley.* Indianapolis: Historical Bureau of the Indiana Library and Historical Department, 1930.

Starr, George W. *Industrial Development of Indiana.* Edited by George W. Starr, *Indiana Studies in Business.* Bloomington: Indiana University School of Business Administration, 1937.

Stegner, Wallace. *Beyond the Hundredth Meridian: John Wesley Powell and the Second Opening of the West.* Lincoln: University of Nebraska Press, 1982.

Sutter, Paul S. *Driven Wild: How the Fight against Automobiles Launched the Modern Wilderness Movement.* Seattle: University of Washington Press, 2002.

Talbott, J. T. *Talbott's Logansport and Peru Directory for 1859–1860.* Indianapolis: J. T. Talbott, 1860.

Uncommon Ground. Edited by William Cronon. New York: W. W. Norton, 1995.

Visher, Stephen S. *Economic Geography of Indiana.* New York: D. Appleton, 1923.

Wabash & Erie Canal in Miami County and in Portions of Wabash and Cass Counties. Edited by Carolyn I. Schmidt. Fort Wayne: Canal Society of Indiana, 2000.

Ward, Robert Wallace. *The Wabash and Erie Canal: A Beautiful Dream.* Privately printed, 1983.

West, Elliot. *The Contested Plains: Indians, Goldseekers, and the Rush to Colorado.* Lawrence: University Press of Kansas, 1998.

White, Richard. *The Organic Machine: The Remaking of the Columbia River.* New York: Hill and Wang, 1995.

Worster, Donald. *Rivers of Empire: Water, Aridity, and the Growth of the American West.* New York: Pantheon Books, 1985.

Index

Page numbers with *italic "n"* or *"nn"* indicate references to footnotes

Page numbers with *italic "ill"* indicate references to maps, photos, or illustrations

A

Adams, John Quincy, 31

agricultural economy, raise of, 63–65

Agricultural History (journal), "Rural Indiana in Transition, 1850–1860," 25*n*54, 58*n*150, 64*n*168

agricultural society, Native Americans as, 11

Allen County, 26–27, 28

American Political Science Review, on establishment of flood districts, 108*n*261

American settlers. *see also* white settlers, vs. Native Americans view of Wabash River, 9

American traders
Ewing family as, 25
extending credit to Native Americans, 24
Miami Nation dependence on, 18–19

animals, impact on canal, 56

annual "freshet," 81

Annual Report of the Chief of Engineers (US Government Printing Office), 79*n*199

annuity payments
Joseph Holman disbursement of Indian, 28
to Miami Nation under Treaty of Paradise Springs (1826), 23–24

The Archaeology of the Whitewater Valley (Setzler), 10*n*12

Army Corps of Engineers
breaking ground for Mississinewa dam project, 111
Fact Sheet: *Mississinewa Dam Safety Project*, 112*n*273
formulating plan for flood control in Peru, 109
Indianapolis North Flood Damage Reduction Project, 97*n*237, 99*n*242

Asdall, Alton A., "Vegetation and Environment," 55*n*139

B

Battle of Fallen Timbers (1794), 16

Bearss, Daniel, 40

Beasley, Al. D., *Twentieth Century Peru*, 93*n*228

Bemis, Samuel Flagg, 17*n*31

Benke, Arthur C., *Rivers of North America*, 12*n*18, 65*n*173

"Beyond the Hundredth Meridian" (*Environmental History*), 15*n*26

Black Hawk, chief of Sac tribe, 14

Blackford, Glen A., *The John Tipton Papers*, 27*n*63, 28*n*65, 31*n*76

Bodurtha, Arthur L.
  on businessmen Bearss and Cole, 40*n*93
  on construction of Wabash and Erie Canal, 34*n*85
  on drainage ditches in Miami County, 78*n*196
  on drainage of land, 66–67, 67*n*179
  economic impact on Peru of railroads, 72*nn*182–83
  on first canal boat going to Peru, 47*n*114
  flood of 1875 in writing of, 83
  on flood of 1883, 85
  on flood of 1913, 98, 102*n*248, 106–7*nn*256–57
  History of Miami County, 10*n*11
  on Hood, 26*n*61, 35*n*90
  on impact on Peru of Wabash and Erie Canal, 49*n*118–19
  on law forfeiting land for delinquent taxes, 59, 59*n*151
  on Miamisport, 32*n*80
  on Mound Builders, 10*n*11
  on population in 1904 of Peru, 90*n*221
  on population in 1913 of Peru, 95*n*233
  providing written history of Peru, 6

  on purchase of land by Joseph Holman and Hood, 33*n*82
  on relationship of Joseph Holman and Hood, 30*n*73
  on Richardville, 20, 20*n*41, 31*n*77

Booth factory (Oakdale), 103

Boyd's Park, 13

bridges, 72

Britton, Richard L., 36, 40

Broadway (Peru), 90*ill*

Broadway Bridge (South Peru)
  in flood of 1913, 102
  opening up South Peru, 72

Brown, Robert M., "The Ohio River Floods of 1913," 109*n*264

Bulletin of the American Geographical Society, "The Ohio River Floods of 1913," 109*n*264

Business History Review, "Entrepreneurship and Western Development," 42*n*99

businesses
  dependence on water power, 72
  losses in flood of 1913, 106

C

Cadillac Desert (Reisner), 107*n*258

Canal Street (Peru), 50, 57, 74, 90*ill*

canals. *see also* Wabash and Erie Canal
  advantages of railroads over, 71
  as dividing line between old and new perception of, 52
  as dumps, 61
  funding on Wabash River of, 16
  impact of nature on, 52
  plans to build from Indianapolis to Mississinewa River, 31
  US leaders view of, 15–16

Carter, Harvey L., "Rural Indiana in Transition, 1850–1860," 25*n*54, 58*n*150, 64*n*168

Cass County, 32, 76

Castaldi, Thomas E.
Wabash & Erie Canal Notebook I,
16*n*29
Wabash & Erie Canal Notebook III,
45*n*110, 73*n*185

Cha-pine, chief of Miami Nation,
46–47, 68

Chesapeake & Ohio, 88–89, 88*ill*

cholera outbreaks, 60–61

circus, losses in flood of 1913, 101–2

Colbert E. Cushing, *Rivers of North
America*, 12*n*18

Cole, Alphonso, 40

*Collections of the Kansas State Historical
Society* (Martin), 61*n*160

Columbia River
damming of, 4
energy of, 12

Congress, passing bill to replace bridge
(1913), 108–9, 109*n*263

The Contested Plains (West), 3, 22*n*48,
29*n*69, 33*n*84

Coppernoll, Marilyn, *Miami County,
Indiana*, 72*n*184

corn, raised by Native Americans in
Peru area, 11

credit, traders extending to Native
Americans, 24

crime
canal bringing Peru, 58–59
in Peru, 58–59

Cronon, William
Nature's Metropolis, 14, 14*n*24,
50*n*125
"The Trouble with Wilderness," 2–3,
2*n*2, 5*n*10, 115, 115*n*275

Cushing, Colbert E., *Rivers of North
America*, 12*n*18, 65*n*173

D

Daily Chronicle. see Peru Daily Chronicle

Dam Number Three, Feeder, 42, 43*ill*,
44–45, 46

damming
of Columbia River, 4
of Wabash River, 67–68

deaths from flood of 1913, 105–6

deforestation, consequences of, 66

deforestation of watershed, erosion
caused by, 78–79

Delphi (IN), 30, 110

*A Description of the City of Peru, Miami
County, Indiana* (Weaver), 70*n*180,
77*nn*192–93

Deverell, William, *Land of Sunshine*
(ed), 95*n*232

diarrhea outbreaks, 61

Dillon, John Brown, *A History of
Indiana*, 18*n*34

diphtheria outbreaks, 61

disease, along canal, 60–61

dishpan rock, in Wabash River near
Boyd's Park, 13, 22

"The Ditch," 62

Documentary Journal, "Select
Committee of the House of
Representatives," 42*n*98

Donald J. Pisani, "Beyond the
Hundredth Meridian," 15*n*26

Dow works, 88

Dr. Bragg's Fever and Ague Pills, 61

Drainage and Reclamation of Swamp
(Kettleborough), 78*nn*194–95

drainage of land, 66–67, 78

Dresser, Paul, *On the Banks of the
Wabash, Far Away*, 2, 2*n*1

drought, impact on canal, 55

Dukes, Aaron, 88

Dunn, Jacob Piatt, "Executive Journal of Indiana Territory 1800–1816," 18*n*33

E

Early Western Travels, 1748–1846 (Thwaites), 11*n*15

Ecological Monographs, "Vegetation and Environment," 55*n*139

Ecology (journal), "Vegetation of the Drainage-Aeration Classes," 64*n*170

economic development
canal bringing, 58
landscape shaped by, 51

Economic Geography of Indiana (Visher), 71*n*181

economy
impact of floods on, 83, 84, 87, 106–8
impact on Peru of railroads, 71–73
impact on Peru of Wabash and Erie Canal, 48–50, 69
railroads impact on, 89–91
raise of agricultural, 63–65

Eel River, 31

electric plants, 91

The Elements of Railroad Engineering, (Raymond), 75, 75*nn*187–88

Elmwood School (Oakdale), 103

"Entrepreneurship and Western Development" (*Business History Review*), 42*n*99

environment
consequences of humans disturbing, 51
regaining control of, 115

environmental change, consequences to Wabash River of, 65–66

environmental changes, cumulative effect on Wabash River of, 79–80

environmental consequences, of railroad construction, 74–76

environmental control, canal and, 58

Environmental History (journal)
"Beyond the Hundredth Meridian," 15*n*26
"The Trouble with Wilderness," 2*n*2

Erie Canal, Wabash and
in 2012, 115*ill*
abandonment of, 72, 73
advantages of railroads over, 71
aiding westward expansion, 17
call for workers, 39–40
chief engineer of, 41
construction of, 34
as "The Ditch," 62
as dividing line between old and new perception of landscape, 52
as dumps, 61
economic impact of, 69
economic potential of, 33
experiencing unexpected economic difficulties, 51
human interference impact on, 56–57
impact of nature on, 52
impact on Peru, 39, 48–50
as Indiana's version of gold rush, 29
legacy of, 5–6
man-made and natural problems with, 54
problems with, 52–53
purchase of, 88
reaching Peru, 47
shipping corn on, 65
use defining Peru, 114

erosion
caused by deforestation of watershed, 78–79
of landscape, 67

Ewing, Alexander
about, 25
elected as justice of the peace, 26
on first grand jury in Allen County, 27

as land commissioner, 28

Ewing, Charles W., 26

Ewing, Charlotte, 27

Ewing, George W., 25

Ewing, William G., 25, 26

Ewing family, in Wabash Valley, 25–26

"Executive Journal of Indiana Territory 1800–1816" (*Indiana Historical Society Publications* III), 18*n*33

F

Fatout, Paul, *Indiana Canals*, 16*n*28, 49*n*122, 56*n*143, 59

Federal Land Office, in Fort Wayne, 24

Feeder Dam Number Three, 42, 43*ill*, 44–45, 46, 69, 72, 73

Fetter, Frank, 33

Fiege, Mark
  as historian, 2
  Irrigated Eden, 4–5, 5*n*7, 51*n*126, 114*n*274

Fisher, Stearns, 34

flood(s)
  1847 vs. 1883, 86–87
  of 1858, 53
  of 1875, 81–84, 81*ill*
  of 1883, 84–88
  of 1904, 91–94
  of 1907, 94–95
  of 1913, 6, 69–70, 97–105
  of 1913, aftermath from, 105–9
  of 1943, 110
  of 1959, 1–2, 112
  as commodity, 52
  challenging perception that humans were in control, 80, 80*n*201
  changing view of, 85
  consideration of railroads on, 74–75
  dates of, 80*n*201
  formation of flood prevention association, 110, 111*ill*

National Weather Service records on, 79–80

prevention vs. control of, 111–12

vulnerability of Peru to, 67–68

Ford, Robert Wallace, 58

Fort Wayne during the Canal Era (Poinsatte), 31*n*79

Fort Wayne (IN)
  businesses development and politics in, 25–29
  canal's impact on, 30
  Ewing family businesses in, 25
  Indian annuities disbursed at, 18–19
  Miami Nation isolated from, 16
  Peru's population vs., 49
  as trading center of Wabash Valley, 20, 23–24

Fort Wayne Sentinel, on disease along canal, 61*n*159

"freshet," annual, 81

G

Gammon, James R., *The Wabash River Ecosystem*, 56*n*140, 64*nn*171–72, 65*n*175

Godfroy, Clarence, chief of Miami Nation
  Miami Indian Stories, 13, 13*n*
  Treaty of Paradise Springs (1826) and, 22

Goodrich, DeWitt C., 61

"The Great Nation of Futurity" (*The United States Democratic Review*), 44*n*106

gristmill rock, in Wabash River near Boyd's Park, 13, 22

Griswold, Bert Joseph
  on Alexander Ewing, 25, 25*n*55
  on Henry Hay at Fort Wayne, 20, 20*n*40
  on James Riley, 23–24, 23–24*nn*51–53

on Joseph Holman, 27, 27*n*64,
28*nn*66–67
*The Pictorial History of Fort Wayne,
Indiana*, 20*n*40
on William Nesbitt Hood, 27*n*62

H

Harrison, General (War of 1812), 25,
27
Hay, Henry, 20
health problems, along canal, 60–62
Hise, Greg, *Land of Sunshine* (ed),
95*n*232
History of Cass County, Indiana (Powell),
97*n*235
A History of Indiana (Dillon), 18*n*34
History of Miami County (Bodurtha),
10*n*11
History of Miami County Indiana (Brant
and Fuller, eds)
on beginning of first real estate boom
in Wabash River area, 33*n*83
on civilization in Peru, 50*nn*123–24
on growth of Miami County, 65*n*174
on Hood, 26*n*60
on impact of dam on Peru, 41*n*96,
42*n*97
on Joseph Holman, 28*n*68, 30*n*74
on Miami County, 64*n*169
on Miamisport, 35*n*88, 36*n*91
as Peru as small village, 44*n*103
on Peru's population vs. Fort Wayne,
49*n*120
on population growth of Peru,
76*n*191
providing written history of Peru, 6
History of Miami County (Stephens),
21*n*45, 31*n*75, 35*n*89, 49*n*121,
66*n*178, 73*n*186
Holman, Joseph
about, 24–25, 27–28
accusing Williams of corruption, 42

leaving Miami County, 36
promoting self-interest, 28–29
relationship to Hood, 32–34
as speculators and supporters of canal,
30–31
support of Miamisport as county seat,
35
view of Wabash River, 37, 113
Holman, Omer, 100
Holman, Solomon, 28
Holman Street School (Peru), 103
Hood, William Nesbitt
about, 24–25
believing man could harness nature
for economic gain, 70
holding first land sale in Peru, 40
imagined Peru as safe location, 83
layout of new town on his land,
34–35
promoting self-interest, 28–29
relationship to Joseph Holman,
32–34
as speculators and supporters of canal,
30
support of Peru as county seat, 35–37
view of Wabash River, 37, 113
Howe, Daniel Wait, "Executive Journal
of Indiana Territory 1800–1816,"
18*n*33
Howe Sewing Machine Company, 72,
82, 83
human interference, impact on canal,
56
humanity vs. nature, 3
Hundley, Will M., *Squawtown*, 66,
66*n*176
Huntington County, 30, 34, 46, 88,
110

I

ice dams, from flood of 1883, 85, 87
illnesses, along canal, 60–61

immigrants, influx to Wabash Valley of, 39, 64

Indian Affairs (Kappler, ed), 22*n*49

Indian Agency, 31

Indian annuities
Joseph Holman disbursement of, 28
to Miami Nation under Treaty of Paradise Springs (1826), 23–24

Indiana (IN)
establishment of flood districts, 108
land grant along Wabash River, 29–30
statehood of, 16
version of gold rush, 29

Indiana (packet boat), 47–48, 52

Indiana Canals (Fatout), 16*n*28, 49*n*122, 56*n*143, 59*nn*152–54

Indiana Constitutional Convention (1816), 28

Indiana Geological Survey (Indiana Dept of Geology and Natural Resources), 66*n*177

Indiana Historical Society Publications III, "Executive Journal of Indiana Territory 1800–1816," 18*n*33

Indiana House of Representatives, "Select Committee of the House of Representatives," 42*n*98

Indiana Manufacturing Company, 83, 87, 96, 98–101, 99*ill*, 106

Indiana Railroad Commission, 110

Indiana Territory, creation of, 17

Indianapolis (IN), 31

Indianapolis News, on flood of 1907, 94*n*231

Indianapolis North Flood Damage Reduction Project (US Army Corps of Engineers), 98, 99*n*242

Indianapolis-Peru railroad, 73

Industrial Development of Indiana (Starr), 76*n*190

industry, introduction of modern, 90–91

Iroquois, war with Miami Nation, 12

Irrigated Eden (Fiege), 4–5, 5*n*7, 51*n*126, 114*n*274

irrigation, from Snake River, 4

J

Jackson, Andrew, 28

Jay's Treaty (Bemis), 17*n*31

John Tipton Papers (Blackford), 31*n*76

The John Tipton Papers (Blackford, ed), 27*n*63

Journal of Economic History
"Midwestern Industrialization," 48*n*117
"State Policy and the Public Domain," 29*n*71

K

Kappler, Charles J., *Indian Affairs* (ed), 22*n*49

Kekionga (Miami village), 19

Kelman, Ari
as historian, 2
A River and Its City, 3–4, 3*n*4, 57*n*146, 61*n*158, 62, 62*n*162, 84*n*210

Kentucky (packet boat), 55

Kettleborough, Charles, *Drainage and Reclamation of Swamp*, 78*nn*194–95

L

Lafayette (IN), 30, 50, 88

Lake Erie & Western Railroad, 88–89, 88*ill*

Land of Sunshine (Deverell and Hise, eds), 95*n*232

land ownership, for Black Hawk, 14

land speculators
  in Miami County, 58–59
  in Wabash Valley, 24–25
landscape
  acceptance of floods as part of
    natural, 94–95
  canal as dividing line between old and
    new perception of, 52
  cause of flood of 1913 caused by
    human manipulation of, 109, 110
  connected to people, 2–3
  consequences of deforestation, 66
  controlling with technology, 69–70
  controls of, 91
  effects of clearing, 64–65
  entangled in meaning, 5
  erosion of, 67
  humans assumption of controlling
    and manipulating water and, 112
  humans attempt to control, 114
  Miami Nation relationship to, 46–47
  owners separation from nature and,
    50–51
  separating from while changing, 62
  shaped by economic development,
    51–52
"Letter from Sylvia to Joe" (Miami
  County Historical Society),
  102n250
Leverett, Frank, *Water Resources of
  Indiana and Ohio*, 79n198
Lindsey, Alton A., "Vegetation of the
  Drainage-Aeration Classes," 64n170
Lindsey, Robert O., "Vegetation and
  Environment," 55n139
Linzee, Jacob, 48
Little Turtle, chief of Miami Nation, 19
*Lives and Works of Civil and Military
  Engineers of America* (Stuart), 41n95,
  45n108, 47n113
Lock Number Nineteen (east end of
  Canal Street), 57
Logansport (IN), 30, 31, 53

Logansport Canal Telegraph
  advertising mill site, 43n101
  call for canal workers, 39–40
  call for canal workers in, 40n92
Lutheran School (Peru), 103

M

"Man in the Middle," 21
Manifest Destiny
  idea of, 115
  of Peru, 77
Manifest Destiny (Moriarty, J. T.),
  44n107
man-made problems, and natural
  problems with canal, 54
man-made vs. natural, 7–8
Martin, George W., *Collections of the
  Kansas State Historical Society*,
  61n160
Maumee River, 19
Mays, Roma B., 105
Meyer, David R., "Midwestern
  Industrialization," 48n117
Miami County
  agriculture within, 63–65
  businessman interested in, 32
  creation of, 34
  on drainage ditches in, 78
  economic output of, 76
  first inhabitants of, 10
  growth of, 65
  Peru chosen as seat of, 35
Miami County Historical Society,
  "Letter from Sylvia to Joe," 102n250
Miami County, Indiana (Coppernoll),
  72n184
Miami County Recorder, "Plat of Mill
  Lots at Peru," 43n102
Miami County Sentinel
  ad for sealed bid on waterwheel in,
  52, 52n129

on aftermath of flood of 1913, 108, 108*n*259–60

on canal as "The Ditch," 62*n*163

on cholera outbreak, 60, 60*nn*156–57

on Dr. Bragg's Fever and Ague Pills, 61*n*161

on flood of 1875, 81–82*nn*202–6

on flood of 1907, 94, 94*n*230

on formation of flood prevention association, 110*n*269

on formulating plan for flood control, 109*n*266–67

on launching of *Peruvian*, 60, 60*n*155

an Peru as "the favored spot of creation," 62–63, 62–63*nn*164–67

Miami Indian Stories (Godfroy), 13*n*

The Miami Indians of Indiana (Rafert), 11*n*16

Miami Nation. *see also* Native Americans

annuity payments to Miami Nation under Treaty of Paradise Springs (1826), 23–24

dependence on American traders, 18–19

footprint on Wabash Valley, 64

inhabiting area of Peru, 9–10, 11

isolation and weakening of, 17–19

relationship to landscape, 46–47

under Richardville, 19–21

spiritual relationship to Wabash River, 12–13, 13, 14

treaties with federal government affecting land along Wabash River, 16

treatment of Wabash River, 37

Treaty of Greenville (1795), 16–17

Treaty of Paradise Springs (1826), 22–23

Treaty of St. Mary's, Ohio (1818), 18

war with Iroquois, 12

weakening and isolation of, 17–19

Miamisport (IN), 30, 31–36, 42, 67

"Midwestern Industrialization" (*Journal of Economic History*), 48*n*117

mills, construction of, 43

Mississinewa dam project (1967), 111–12

Mississinewa Dam Safety Project, Fact sheet (US Army Corps of Engineers), 112*n*273

Mississinewa River

confluence of Wabash and Mississinewa Rivers blocked by railbed, 88–89, 88*ill*

dam build at Peru, 110

flood of 1883 and, 85

impact of railroads on, 71

plans to build canal from Indianapolis to, 31

prehistoric artifacts along, 11

treaties with US affecting land along, 17

Mississippi River, vs. New Orleans, 3–4

Monroe, James, 24, 28

Moriarty, J. T., *Manifest Destiny*, 44*n*107

Mound Builders

footprint on Wabash Valley, 64

inhabiting area of Peru, 9, 10–11

N

National Hotel (Peru), 47

National Road, 17

National Weather Service records, on floods in Peru, 79–80, 79*n*200

Native Americans. *see also* Miami Nation

vs. American settlers view of Wabash River, 9

annuity payments to Miami Nation under Treaty of Paradise Springs (1826), 23–24

defeated at Battle of Fallen Timbers (1794), 16

footprint on Wabash Valley, 64
idea of land ownership, 14
inhabiting area of Peru, 9–10, 11
Miami Nation war with Iroquois, 12
relationship to landscape, 46–47
respecting power of Wabash River, 14
spiritual relationship to Wabash
   River, 12–13
traders extending credit to, 24
treaties with federal government
   affecting land along Wabash and
   Mississinewa Rivers, 16–17
treatment of Wabash River, 37
Treaty of Greenville (1795), 16–17
Treaty of Paradise Springs (1826), 20,
   22–23
Treaty of St. Mary's, Ohio (1818), 18
using rock in Wabash River, 13
in Wabash Valley, 7
natural gas, 72
natural problems
   as largest thread to canal, 54–55
   and man-made problems with canal,
   54
natural vs. man-made, 7–8
nature
   consequences when humans attempt
      to alter, 113–14
   existing to be conquered, 44
   vs. humanity, 3
   technology and, 68, 114
Nature's Metropolis (Cronon), 14,
   14n24, 50n125
New Orleans
   illnesses from crews from, 60–61
   vs. Mississippi River, 3–4
   yellow fever epidemic of 1853, 4
Northwest Territories, 15

O

Oakdale (IN), 93, 103, 107
"The Ohio River Floods of 1913"
   *(Bulletin of the American
   Geographical Society)*, 109n264
oil and natural gas, discovery of, 91
On the Banks of the Wabash, Far Away
   (Dresser), 2n1
The Organic Machine (White), 4n5,
   12n21, 51n128, 75n189, 90n222
O'Sullivan, John, "The Great Nation of
   Futurity," 44, 44n106

P

Palmer, Tim, *The Snake River*, 56n142
Panic of 1837, 48
Paradise Spring Treaty (1826), 20,
   22–23, 29
people, connected to natural landscape,
   2–3
people's interference, impact on canal,
   56
Peru (IN), 76*ill*
   1847 vs. 1883 floods, 86–87
   Canal Street in, 50
   chosen as county seat, 35–36
   connection between Wabash River
      and, 113
   construction of mills in, 43
   crime in, 58–59
   dam build at Peru, 110
   economic shift in, 48–50, 58
   establishment of, 36–37
   establishment of flood district in, 108
   as "the favored spot of creation,"
      62–63
   flood of 1875, 81–84, 81*ill*
   flood of 1883, 84–88
   flood of 1904, 91–94
   flood of 1907, 94–95
   flood of 1913, 6, 97–105, 103*ill*
   flood of 1913, aftermath from, 105–9

flood of 1959, 1–2, 112
formulating plan for flood control, 109–10
growth of, 39
growth of population in, 43–44
impact of floods on economy, 83, 84, 87, 106–8
impact of railroads on, 71–73
inhabitants in area of, 9–11
introduction of modern industry in, 90–91
land owners separation from nature in, 50–51
legacy of Wabash River and Erie Canal to, 5–6
Manifest Destiny of, 77
Mound Builders inhabiting, 9, 10–11
naming of, 35
Native Americans inhabiting, 9–11, 16–17
population growth of, 76, 90, 95
promotion of flood control efforts at, 110, 111*ill*
as rail and business center, 76
railbed as dam at confluence of Wabash and Mississinewa Rivers blocked by railbed, 88–89, 88*ill*
railroads impact on, 71–72
separating from Wabash River, 77–78
use of water defining, 114
vulnerability to floods, 67–68
Wabash and Erie Canal reaching, 47
white settlers inhabiting, 10, 15, 18, 30
Peru & Indianapolis Railroad, 71–72
Peru Brewery, 66
Peru Daily Chronicle
on flood of 1904, 92–93, 92*n*2245, 93*nn*226–27
on flood of 1907, 94, 94*n*229
Peru Daily Tribune
on end of three-dam project, 111*n*271
on repairs to Mississinewa dam, 112*n*272
Peru Evening Journal, on flood of 1913, 100, 100*n*244, 100*n*246, 104–5*nn*252–55, 110*n*268
Peru Forester (newspaper)
advertising goods from New York, 48, 48*n*116
Indiana going on canal to Peru, 47
Peru Observer
on blame for delay in opening canal, 56–57, 57*nn*144–45
on breaks in canal, 53, 53*n*134
on packet boat *Kentucky* swept through breach, 55*n*136
Peru Republican
on cause of flood of 1883, 84–85
on flood of 1883, 85–88, 85*nn*212–13, 86*nn*216–17, 87–88*nn*218–20
on flood of 1904, 92, 92*nn*223–24
on flood of 1913, 98*nn*238–40, 99*n*243, 100, 100*n*245, 101–2, 102*n*247, 102*n*249, 104*n*251
on formulating plan for flood control, 109*n*265
on impact of flood of 1875, 83*nn*208–9
on Shirk, 96*n*234
Peru Republican (newspaper), on breaks in canal, 53*nn*131–33
The Peru Sentinel, on flood of 1875, 82
Peruvian (boat), 60
The Pictorial History of Fort Wayne, Indiana (Griswold and Taylor), 20*n*40. *see also* Griswold, Bert Joseph
"Plat of Mill Lots at Peru" (Miami County Recorder), 43*n*102
Poinsatte, Charles R., *Fort Wayne during the Canal Era*, 31*n*79
population growth, 49, 76, 90, 95
Potawatomi tribe, 16, 17, 37

Powell, Jehu Z., *History of Cass County, Indiana*, 97*n*235

Pratt, Daniel, 72

prehistoric mound builders, inhabiting area of Peru, 9, 10–11

puddle, using, 52

R

Rae, John Bell, "Federal Land Grants in Aid of Canals," 30*n*72

Rafert, Stewart
on Ewing family experience as traders, 25
on John Tipton, 25*n*56
The Miami Indians of Indiana, 11*n*16
on Miami Nation, 12*n*17, 16*n*30, 18*n*35, 19*nn*36–37
on Treaty of Paradise Springs (1826), 22, 22*n*50

railbed as dam, at confluence of Wabash and Mississinewa Rivers blocked by railbed, 88–89, 88*ill*

railroad construction, environmental consequences of, 74–76

railroads, 74*ill*
consideration of flooding by, 74–75
emergence of, 70–71
impact on economy, 89–91
impact on Peru of, 71–73

rains, impact on canal, 55

Rascally Scrambling Trade, 20*n*40

Raymond, William Galt, *The Elements of Railroad Engineering,*, 75, 75*nn*187–88

Reisner, Marc
Cadillac Desert, 107, 107*n*258
as historian, 2

Richardville, Jean Baptiste, chief of Miami Nation, 19–21, 31

Riley, James, 23–24

A River and Its City (Kelman), 3–4, 3*n*4, 57*n*146, 61*n*158, 62*n*162, 84*n*210

rivers
overlooked, 2
part in westward expansion of settlers, 15
US leaders view of, 15–16

Rivers of North America (Cushing and Benke), 12*n*18, 65*n*173

rock, in Wabash River near Boyd's Park, 13, 22

"Rural Indiana in Transition, 1850–1860" (*Agricultural History*), 25*n*54, 58*n*150, 64*n*168

S

Salamonie River, 110

Scheiber, Harry N.
"Entrepreneurship and Western Development," 42*n*99
"State Policy and the Public Domain," 29*n*71

Schmidt, Carolyn I., *"Wabash & Erie Canal in Miami County,"* 45*n*111, 55*n*138, 57*nn*147–48

settlers. *see* white settlers

Setzler, Frank M., 10–11, 10*n*12

Shields, Delight, 104

Shirk, Elbert W., 96, 96*ill*, 97, 98–101, 106

Shirk, Milton, 88

sickness, along canal, 60–61

Smith's Island (IN), in flood of 1913, 103

Snake River, irrigation from, 4

The Snake River (Palmer), 51*n*127, 56*n*142

South Peru (IN)
flood of 1875, 82
flood of 1904, 91

flood of 1913, 99–100, 104, 104*ill*, 105, 105*ill*, 106*ill*
flood prevention in, 95
opening up of, 72
spiritual relationship to Wabash River, Miami Nation, 12–13
Squawtown (Hundley), 66*n*176
St. Joseph River, 19
St. Mary's River, 19
Starr, George W., *Industrial Development of Indiana*, 76*n*190
Stephens, Charles, 6
Stephens, John H., *History of Miami County*, 21*n*45, 31*n*75, 32, 32*n*81, 35*n*89, 49*n*121, 66, 66*n*178, 73*n*186
Sterling, David K., "Vegetation and Environment," 55*n*139
Stuart, Charles B., *Lives and Works of Civil and Military Engineers of America*, 41*n*95, 45*n*108, 47*n*113
swampland, drainage of, 78

T

taverns, fights at waterfront centered on, 59–60
Taylor, Samuel R., *The Pictorial History of Fort Wayne, Indiana*, 20*n*40
technology, nature and, 68
technology controlling landscape, 69–70, 112, 114
Thwaites, Reuben Gold, *Early Western Travels, 1748–1846*, 11*n*15
Tim Palmer, *The Snake River*, 51*n*127
Tipton, John, 20, 25, 26, 28, 31, 32
traders
Ewing family as, 25
extending credit to Native Americans, 24
Miami Nation dependence on American, 18–19

transcontinental railroad, 45
transportation
movement to modernize, 78
transformation of landscape with new methods of, 17
Treaty of Greenville (1795), 16
Treaty of Paradise Springs (1826), 20, 22–23, 29
Treaty of St. Mary's, Ohio (1818), 18
"The Trouble with Wilderness" (Cronon), 2*n*2, 5*n*10, 115*n*275
Twentieth Century Peru (Beasley), 93*n*228

U

The United States Democratic Review, "The Great Nation of Futurity," 44*n*106
United States (US)
leaders view of rivers and canals, 15–16
treaties with Native Americans affecting land along Mississinewa River, 17
treaties with Native Americans affecting land along Wabash River, 16, 17
Treaty of Greenville (1795), 16–17
Treaty of Paradise Springs (1826), 20, 22–23, 29
Treaty of St. Mary's, Ohio (1818), 18
US Army Corps of Engineers
breaking ground for Mississinewa dam project, 111
Fact Sheet: *Mississinewa Dam Safety Project*, 112*n*273
formulating plan for flood control in Peru, 109
Indianapolis North Flood Damage Reduction Project, 97*n*237, 99*n*242
US Congress, passing bill to replace bridge (1913), 108–9, 109*n*263

US Department of the Interior, on
flood of 1913, 97n236

US Geologic Service, on flood of 1913,
97

US Geological Survey (1896), effect of
settlement on Wabash River, 78–79

US Government Printing Office,
*Annual Report of the Chief of
Engineers*, 79n199

US Senate, Flood Control Act of 1958,
110, 110n270

V

Van, Willard, "Vegetation and
Environment," 55n139

vegetation, impact on canal, 55

"Vegetation and Environment"
(Ecological Monographs), 55n139

"Vegetation of the Drainage-Aeration
Classes," 64n170

Visher, Stephen S., *Economic Geography
of Indiana*, 71n181

W

Wabash, St. Louis, & Pacifiic Railway,
72

Wabash & Erie Canal 1847 (Williams),
45n109

"*Wabash & Erie Canal in Miami
County*" (Schmidt), 45n111,
55n138, 57nn147–48

Wabash & Erie Canal Notebook I
(Castaldi), 16n29

Wabash & Erie Canal Notebook III
(Castaldi), 45n110, 73n185

Wabash and Erie Canal
in 2012, 115*ill*
abandonment of, 72, 73
advantages of railroads over, 71
aiding westward expansion, 17

call for workers, 39–40
chief engineer of, 41
construction of, 34
as "The Ditch," 62–63
as dividing line between old and new
perception of landscape, 52
as dumps, 61
economic impact of, 69
economic potential of, 33
environmental control and, 58
experiencing unexpected economic
difficulties, 51
human interference impact on, 56–57
impact of nature on, 52
impact on Peru, 39, 48–50
as Indiana's version of gold rush, 29
legacy of, 5–6
man-made and natural problems
with, 54
natural problems as largest thread to,
54–56
problems with, 52–53
purchase of, 88
reaching Peru, 47
shipping corn on, 65
use defining Peru, 114

The Wabash and Erie Canal (Ward),
52n130, 54n135, 55n137, 56n141,
58n149

Wabash County, 30, 34, 76, 110

Wabash Railroad, 88–89, 88*ill*

Wabash River
bridge over, 72
changes in 1820s along, 29
confluence of Wabash and
Mississinewa Rivers blocked by
railbed, 88–89, 88*ill*
connection between Peru and, 113
consequences of environmental
change, 65–66
cumulative effect of environmental
changes on, 79–80
damming of, 67–68
flooding of. *see* flood(s)

formulating plan for flood control
along, 109–10
funding of canals on, 16
ice dams from flood of 1883 on, 85,
87
impact of drainage of land on, 67
modern industry and, 91
Native Americans vs. American
settlers view, 9
origins of name of, 12, 12n19
people disconnected from, 51
prehistoric artifacts along, 11
process of reimagining, 29
rock near Boyd's Park in, 13, 22
separating from Peru, 77–78
treatment by Native Americans of, 37
Treaty of Paradise Springs (1826)
impact on, 23
The Wabash River Ecosystem (Gammon),
56n140, 64nn171–72, 65n175
Wabash Rivers, impact of railroads on,
71
"Wabash Shakes," 61
Wabash Valley
influx of immigrants to, 39, 64
land speculators in, 24–25
Native American societies in, 7
occupants seeing river differently
because of canal, 51
topography of upper, 14
white immigrants in, 7
Wallace, Ben, 101, 101*ill*
War of 1812, 25, 27
Ward, Robert Wallace, *The Wabash
and Erie Canal*, 52n130, 54n135,
55n137, 56n141, 58n149
Washington, George, 15–16
water. *see also* flood(s), as commodity,
52
Water Resources of Indiana and Ohio
(Leverett), 79n198
waterwheel, ad for sealed bid on, 52

Weaver, Clarence E., *A Description of the
City of Peru, Miami County, Indiana*,
70, 77nn192–93
weeds, impact on canal, 56
West, Elliot, *The Contested Plains*, 3,
3n3, 21–22, 22n48, 29, 29n69, 33,
33n84
Western Seaman's Friend Society, 59
White, Richard
as historian, 2
The Organic Machine, 4, 4n5, 5, 12,
12n21, 14, 51, 51n128, 75n189,
90n222
White Raccoon (Indian Village), 46
white settlers
along Wabash River, 30
inhabiting area of Peru, 10, 15,
17–18, 30
manipulation of Wabash River, 14
in Miamisport, 33
vs. Native Americans view of Wabash
River, 9
view of Wabash River, 13
in Wabash Valley, 7, 25
westward expansion of, 15
Whittemore form, 75
Williams, Jesse L., 41*ill*
about, 45
on canal structures, 57
as chief engineer of Wabash and Erie
Canal, 34, 36, 40–42, 68
view of Dam Number Three, 45–46
Wabash & Erie Canal 1847, 45n109
Winter, George, 64, 67
Woollen, William Wesley, "Executive
Journal of Indiana Territory 1800–
1816," 18n33

Y

yellow fever epidemic of 1853 (New
Orleans), 4